For Priscilla

from

Helen.

ESSAYS ON GERMAN INFLUENCE UPON ENGLISH EDUCATION AND SCIENCE
1850 - 1919

CONNECTICUT COLLEGE MONOGRAPH NO. 9

Essays on German Influence upon English Education and Science,

1850 - 1919

by

GEORGE HAINES IV (1903–1964)

CONNECTICUT COLLEGE
in association with
ARCHON BOOKS

Orders should be placed with
ARCHON BOOKS
995 Sherman Avenue
Hamden, Connecticut 06514

SBN 208 00762 8

Library of Congress Catalog Card Number: 68–58409

Printed in the United States of America

To M.W.H.

Contents

Notes follow each chapter.

Foreword

The present volume makes available to scholars some of the last writings of George Haines IV (1903–64). We hope it may also serve as a tribute to the memory of an inspiring teacher and colleague.

George Haines was born in West Chester, Pennsylvania, and his early years were given to managing his family's long established grocery business. During these years he nonetheless found the time to read widely, particularly in modern poetry, and to follow the contemporary arts with keen interest. Even after he had entered upon his professional career, Mr. Haines always retained something of an earlier perspective which transcended all the usual academic categories. When the lessening of family obligations made it possible, he began to prepare for a career of teaching and scholarship. In 1938 he received an A.B. from Swarthmore College, and in 1942 a Ph.D. from the University of Pennsylvania. After one year of teaching English at the Drexel Institute, he joined the Department of History at Connecticut College, where he remained for the rest of his life. In 1955 he was named Charles J. MacCurdy Professor of American History; he served as Chairman of the Department from 1954 through 1957 and from 1960 through 1963.

At Connecticut College, Mr. Haines quickly made his mark as an extraordinary teacher, and his course in the Cultural History of Modern Europe had for many years an important influence on the thinking of the whole College community. His research interests lay largely within the same area of modern cultural history, and he gradually came to focus his primary attention on the problem of German influence on England in the nineteenth and twentieth centuries[1]. In 1957 he published a book *German Influence*

[1]For a list of the principal publications of George Haines IV, see Appendix I.

upon English Education and Science, 1800–1866 (Connecticut College Monograph, No. 6, New London, Connecticut), and he followed this with several articles. During his last years, Mr. Haines devoted himself to the preparation of a general study on the problem which most concerned him, and shortly before his death he completed a manuscript entitled *The German Influence and the Decline of England.*

In the circumstances, it was evident that the question of publication involved difficult decisions, and several of his colleagues undertook to investigate the possibilities. To our regret, it eventually became clear that publication of the entire manuscript, close to a thousand typed pages in length, was not practicable at the moment. We were glad to discover, however, that the chapters dealing with education formed a unity within the larger whole and that they might appear separately as a companion volume to Mr. Haines' earlier book. It is these chapters which are here printed under the title *Essays on German Influence upon English Education and Science, 1850–1919.* In accord with the intent of the author for the entire manuscript, they have been dedicated to his wife.

We recognize that any such extraction of separate chapters from a larger work involves some loss of continuity and coherence. In order to suggest to the reader the plan and scope of the complete manuscript, a listing of its chapters and sub-chapters may be found in Appendix II. The complete manuscript itself has been deposited in the Palmer Library of Connecticut College, and a microfilm copy is available on inter-library loan.

In the preparation of these *Essays* for the press, we are indebted to Miss Ashley Hibbard, Connecticut College, '67, for valuable help with preliminary indexing of the material, and to Mrs. Boris I. Bittker, of New Haven, for the final styling of the work. Lastly, our thanks go to President Charles E. Shain and to the Trustees of Connecticut College, and to the Department of History at Connecticut College, for subventions which made publication possible.

F. Edward Cranz
Helen F. Mulvey
Lenore O'Boyle

Connecticut College

ESSAYS ON GERMAN INFLUENCE UPON
ENGLISH EDUCATION AND SCIENCE
1850 - 1919

Germany and England after 1850

What has been called the age of nationalism and realism wit-
nessed the apogee of the Franco-British influence in Europe. By
1850 the German Awakening seemed to have spent its force. Even
in Germany it appeared to have waned; in the universities of the
Continent as well as of England, English empiricism and French
positivism were in the ascendent. Not only had the predominant
flow of cultural influences during the first half of the century continued as throughout the preceding one hundred and fifty years:
from Britain, France, and the Low Countries outward over Europe
and to the rest of the world, but after the mid-century mark, this
movement appeared, if anything, more irresistible than before.

Particularly widespread was the recognition of Britain's supremacy in industry, her leadership in constitutional government, the
genius of her scientists, the economic theories of the classical
school, the psychological theories of the associationists, the logic
of empiricism and induction. All of these enjoyed a wide influence
on the Continent. Faraday, Joule, Frankland, Lyell, Owen, Hooker,
Brown, Darwin, Mill, Spencer, among others, were names of
substantial reputation throughout the world.

Yet the appearances were in many ways deceiving. Under the
surface flowed subsidiary currents where eddies and whirlpools
of thought were gathering strength. And it was in those subsidiary
currents that the German influence was most pronounced, as it
gradually permeated the minds of Englishmen. For far from having
expended its force the German Awakening had merely begun to
exert its influence, as it mixed and mingled with the older stream.

The second phase of the German influence in England began

in the sixties and was characterized by an emphasis on institutional forms, as in the German Awakening. The earlier phase had been pre-eminently intellectual and artistic: many individuals had dipped into the stream of German ideas and forms, taking from their source what each had been able to grasp or had found attractive, but exercising little care in comprehending the totality of any particular philosopher's thought.

During the decades following the Second Reform Bill, various strands of the German influence which had entered England even earlier were being strengthened as more and more Englishmen were influenced by them. At the same time the clerics, aesthetes, and amateurs in things German gave way increasingly to the professionals. No longer was it litterateurs and biblical students who spread the new learning; they were replaced by professional philosophers, historians, philologists, jurists, physicians, and scientists. This is the meaning of the phrase, "the institutionalization of the German influence." Within this phrase are included the professionalization of various disciplines, the introduction of new subjects of study, the creation of schools of thought, as well as changes made in existing English institutions as a result of the German influence. Before tracing this phase in England, however, something of the character of the German institutions, practices, and achievements must be understood.

In a famous essay on the German historians, Lord Acton remarked that in organizing the University of Berlin for the Hohenzollern state of Prussia, Wilhelm von Humboldt had "forged the link between science and force."[1] No lover of force, Acton probably had in mind what was elaborated a few years later by a less critical admirer of the Germans, John Theodore Merz. Born in Manchester of a German father, Merz was educated in German universities, and in his principal work, *A History of European Thought in the Nineteenth Century*, revealed a profound understanding of these institutions. "The German nation," he wrote, "may pride itself on possessing . . . the most powerful and best equipped army . . . With greater pride it may boast of having trained in the course of centuries the largest and most efficient intellectual army, ready at any moment to take up and carry to a successful issue great scientific undertakings demanding the intense thought and labour of a few secluded students or the combined efforts of a large number of ready workers. The army is scattered through the length and breadth of the land . . ." That his comparison of the German organization of learning and the sciences to an army was not merely a chance metaphor is indicated by a later comment. "Wherever the progress of learning and science requires a large amount of detailed study inspired by a few leading ideas, or subservient to some common design and plan, the German universities and higher schools supply a well-trained army of workers, standing under the intellectual generalship of a few great leading minds."[2]

Merz was not original in his use of this metaphor; it appeared frequently in the same context in the addresses of the English scientists in the seventies and eighties. But suggestive as the metaphor is, it yet fails to elucidate the essential characteristics of the German system. In what new sense, one inquires, had learning become power?

Any study, any concentrated concern with theory, may be of intellectual interest, but intellectual interests are of social importance only as they become the guides or auxiliaries of social action. The sciences, taken simply as investigations into the truths of nature, or as long as they remain intellectual adventures, have their effects only in an indirect and delayed fashion. Their social effect or social power is immensely augmented when they enter directly into or affect immediately the way we do things.

In the mid-twentieth century the tremendous power generated by technologies founded on the theoretical sciences hardly needs emphasis. But this sort of power is relatively recent. Though the idea of acquiring power through theoretical scientific knowledge was current in English and Continental thought from at least the time of Bacon and Descartes, and though technological application of scientific theory was frequently, if intermittently, made earlier, only in the nineteenth century did the rate of the transformation of theoretical scientific knowledge into technologies and inventions become sufficiently rapid to be of major importance.[3] The tempo of this process was so remarkably accelerated in the course of the century that A. N. Whitehead declared that the greatest invention of that century of innumerable inventions was "the invention of invention."[4]

Until about the middle decades of the century, invention proceeded side by side with scientific investigations with only occasional over-lappings, occasional cross-fertilizations. The early inventions were largely, though not exclusively, the product of trial-and-error artisans. Science was, on the other hand, the product of independent theoretical speculators and inspired amateur experimenters. But the method of utilizing one in conjunction with the other continuously and purposefully had been but slightly developed. The method of invention implies an organized and systematic investigation of the implications of scientific principles or highly abstract generalities in order to determine their possible applications to specific economic or social ends.[5]

Several things are prerequisite to this. First, there must be a body of established theoretical principles from which the implications can be deduced; during the middle decades of the century a large body of such principles was being established. Second, there must be both a body of sound technical procedures and extensive laboratories for the training of large groups of men in the theoretical principles as well as the standardized experimental procedures. These men are the technologists. From among them a few men of genius may emerge, but for the most part they remain technologists. Since rather less abstract imaginative power is demanded of them than of workers at the highest theoretical level, more can qualify. Working in groups under intelligent direction, tenacity and some imagination will enable them to obtain such results as are possible within any given theoretical framework. During the second and third quarters of the century the technological procedures were being rapidly standardized and laboratories constructed, particularly in the universities of Germany and for the very purpose of founding industries based on the new technologies.[6] Finally, there is required a still larger body of men capable of supervising and applying the newly discovered technics in industry or society at large. These are the technicians, and since less abstract imaginative power is demanded of them than of either of the former groups, even more can qualify. The technologists and technicians are together what, in Merz's words, the German universities and polytechnical schools were especially designed to produce: "a well-trained army of workers, standing under the intellectual generalship of a few great leading minds." The invention of the method of invention was primarily an invention of the Germans.[7]

Early attempts toward developing the method of invention were made by the English, Scots, Dutch, and French, and it was from them, and particularly from the French, that the Germans during the first three decades of the century gained their earliest insights into the method. But it was not a cultural accident that the Germans brought the process to full maturity by organizing and systematizing the hints gathered from abroad, for once understood, the process appears as a characteristic offshoot of the German culture. Our analysis of the requirements of the method discloses how it harmonizes with, and gives strict pertinence to, Merz's metaphor. And if it would be misleading to assert that German culture was organized fundamentally on the model of an army, many, if not most, of the important cultural institutions, especially of Prussia, reflected the organizational imprint of the army, and the army had accustomed the nation to the pattern of hierarchical ranking and systematic gradations of authority and obedience.[8]

When the scientific influences from the West entered the Germanies, the latter were rigidly institutionalized societies. Despite the alterations wrought during the Napoleonic years, the authority of the restored princes, the guilds, the churches, and the universities remained almost untouched. And when a German student, having graduated from a German university, went to Paris for further study, as many did between 1800 and 1830, he returned home to enter upon a career of teaching in a state-supported and supervised university or polytechnic school, becoming thereupon a member of the State's civil service, devoted above all to the interests of the State and with a conscious duty to perform for it.[9]

The bureaucratic civil service, as seen in the Prussian bureaucracy developed in the late seventeenth century to supply the army, may well have been, according to Walter Dorn, "the most enduring achievement of the absolute monarchy," and "survived all the revolutionary changes of the nineteenth century."[10] The same writer defines a bureaucracy as "a hierarchy of appointed, paid and removable civil servants, equipped with definite commissions to perform certain special functions. Its essence is accountability and control. It implies a complicated administrative mechanism based on the principles of division of labor and specialized technical skill."[11] Though the missions a bureaucracy is called upon to perform and the nature of its training are obviously very different from that of an army, the similarity of the structural organization is apparent. As the army in the military, the bureaucracy in civil life represented the model of professional services.

These two great state institutions necessarily exerted a strong impress upon the people, for no German failed to come into continual contact with one or the other. Both inculcated the necessity for training and the advantages of education in a hierarchical order. Both inculcated that respect for titles, rank, and authority so characteristic of the Germans. The rigid class structure operated to a like effect. This was again reflected in the educational system with its lines of division between the *Volksschulen* and continuation or trade schools, the *Realschulen* and higher technical schools, and the gymnasia and universities. Under state supervision and with large state subsidies, with all teachers from the elementary schools through the universities trained members of the state bureaucracy, this carefully graded system was based upon compulsory education to the age of fourteen, followed by two years of military training, and often by subsequent trade or technical instruction.[12]

The systematic gradation of ranks with corresponding duties and responsibilities was promoted also by another important element in German culture: German idealist philosophy. What lay perhaps at the heart of this culture, other than the dynastic will, was an overwhelming conviction of the necessity for order, for systematic arrangement, flowing from an ineradicable faith in the importance of theoretical knowledge as a guide to practice, a faith taught by every major idealist philosopher. As R. B. Haldane declared in an address at Oxford in 1911: "System then, system necessarily in its first aspect abstract, but system that has its beginning and end in concrete life, this was the intellectual inheritance of the German nation from the philosophers and poets of the early nineteenth century."[13]

All of these—the army experience, the bureaucratic regimes, the society, highly structured by class, the carefully designed system of education, a belief in system and the systematic unity of knowledge—contributed to a cultural situation favorable to the invention of the method of invention. For when the German students learned in Leyden, Paris, or Uppsala of the experimental method and with it the need for weight and measure, they sought on their return to their own universities to formalize or systematize this new method of study, to create true disciplines in the German sense (*Wissenschaften*), in which students might be accurately trained to become assistants in research and to train yet others. It was not a mistaken wit who dubbed Justus Liebig's teaching laboratory "a factory for the manufacture of chemists," for that was, in fact, its greatest significance: it was the educational equivalent of mass production in industry. In the eighteenth century the German universities had become schools for the training of the professional administrative bureaucracy; in the nineteenth they became schools for the training of the bureaucracy of professional scientists and scholars.

By the third quarter of the century all the world acknowledged German supremacy in science, technology, and scholarship. To the German university laboratory and seminars went the best students of America, the Continent, and England. The rapidity of Germany's industrial development became one of the world's wonders and it was particularly notable in the industries most dependent upon technology and engineering. The power of the German army was unrivalled. Long before the end of the century the British were well aware of the challenge posed by Germany.

How alien all this was to the England of 1867! By comparison England had nothing remotely deserving the name of a national system of education. Her universities were aggregations of undergraduate colleges. Her numerous original men of science were, except for a few trained on the Continent, brilliant amateurs. Scientifically trained technologists were rare. Only the foundations had been laid for a professional bureaucracy, and there were few recognized professions of any kind. The army, in which commissions were still purchasable, was without a general staff and was hardly an army at all in the Continental sense.

1.

The "atomism" of English empirical liberal society

The "era of reform" of the middle decades of the century represented in Britain an effort to revise the practices and institutions of the past to fulfill the functions required by the complexities of the modern mass society being produced by the new industrial techniques. To a degree this was common to all the nations of the West and to those influenced by western European society. The great political movements of the third quarter of the century were partially an expression of the demand for power and for organization by the middle and lower classes, as well as a demand for freedom from feudal and monarchical restrictions, economic, political, and social.

With the declining influence of the landed aristocracy and their commercial allies and the rise of the industrial middle classes in the course of the eighteenth and early nineteenth century in England, the movement toward liberalizing government became inescapable. But to liberalize government meant almost literally to destroy the monarchical institutional pattern in every sphere of life, a pattern which had constituted the very structure of civilized Europe and its institutional life. The French Revolution was the unmistakable sign that not merely was government to be revised in such a way as to make the subjects of a country into citizens participating in public affairs with all careers open to talent, but also that all the institutions which were the products of aristocratic privilege or royal prerogative, were to be either destroyed or modified beyond recognition.

Because in England the Revolution of 1688 had gone far toward promoting these ends, the English could rightly feel at the beginning of the nineteenth century that they were in many, and in the most important respects, at the forefront in the direction that European society was moving. Though fear of a resurgent France lingered, English ideological sympathies lay with those who in any country sought to attain at least such limitations upon the powers of the dynastic monarchs and the Catholic Church, as had been imposed in Britain, and to attain to such a sense of nationality, political unity, and self-government as they themselves already enjoyed.

Yet even the British had not proceeded far upon the path opened up by the Republican Revolutionaries in France or America. For English Radicals, Dissenters, and manufacturing interests there was much destructive work yet to be done; many vested interests to be destroyed. Many careers remained to be opened to talent rather than to birth or even fortune: the army, the navy, the Church, and the universities were still largely class monopolies and had yet to be attacked. By the end of Gladstone's first administration, however, the axe had been laid to the roots of most of these; by 1874, if the destruction was not already complete, it was well begun.

But even while the realization of the liberal program was being accomplished, doubts concerning it had arisen with ever-increasing force, and more important than the doubts were the consequences of the liberal successes. In the interest of destroying the dynastic institutions, the rallying cry of freedom had sufficed: laissez-faire and laissez-passer; self-interest, voluntary cooperation, and freedom of contract would do the rest. For the most part, the old loyalties, traditions, and institutions dependent on status or privilege, with the exception of the Church, were being questioned or dissolved. The franchise was extended, the Universities opened to dissenters, and army commissions were no longer to be purchased. The reduction of society and social relations to the constituent individuals related only by voluntary, contractual association brought about, as nearly as such a thing is conceivable in a traditionally conscious, complex modern society, that wholly supposititious situation postulated by seventeenth century philosophers as preceding the making of the social contract, men living in a state of nature. And if in the proof some found it approached Rousseau's notion, that men are by nature good and a society almost without compulsory institutional relations ideal, many more certainly discovered life in such circumstances to be closer to Hobbes' conception of it: "solitary, poor, nasty, brutish, and short." The most complete atomization of society occurred in the nineteenth century. "We all live now," wrote J. H. Stirling, "divorced from substance, forlorn each of us, isolated to himself— an absolutely abstract unit in a universal, unsympathising, unparticipant *atomism.*"[14] Or, since that is the testimony of an Hegelian philosopher, here is Beatrice Webb's description of her home in the seventies: "The world of human intercourse in which I was brought up was in fact an endless series of human beings, unrelated one to another, and only casually connected with the family group . . . Our social relations had no roots in neighborhood, in vocation, in creed, or for that matter in race; they likened a series of moving pictures—surface impressions without depth—restlessly stimulating in their glittering variety."[15]

The need for re-integration, for some form of institutionalized relations, resulted in large measure from the liberal triumphs. Not only in England, however, but in all industrialized countries during the last four decades of the nineteenth century, increasing populations, extension of education, greater facility of communication and travel, and the growing intricacy of scientific and technological knowledge and practice resulted in a rapid increase in the institutional complexity of society. Contemporaneously with what may be called the "disintegration of society," wrought by the destruction of the dynastic institutions and by the growing specialization and division of labor, a social re-integration was taking place through the establishment of new institutional ties and a renewal of what remained of the older institutions. When the dynastic organizations of social control, such as the guilds and privileged corporations, including the church establishments, broke down or were compelled to restrict radically their functions, the middle and lower classes began to create new organizations of their own based on the principle of voluntary, contractual association: study societies, professional organizations, limited liability joint stock corporations, trade unions, employers' associations, and many more.

Meanwhile, the results of a policy of laissez-faire in the cities— the vast slums with their mean housing and lack of utilities, the shocking extremes of poverty and wealth, magnified under the favorable industrial conditions of the sixties and early seventies and the depression which followed—invited, indeed made inevitable, intervention by government. No doctrinaire socialism but the streets of Birmingham, his nonconformist conscience, and his experience of business organization led Joseph Chamberlain to inform the Birmingham Council that "All monopolies which are sustained by the State ought to be in the hands of the representatives of the people, by whom they should be administered, and to whom their profits should go."[16] The central government also was being forced into regulating certain private industries. Revenue declines were, in the sixties, pushing the railroads toward working agreements and amalgamations. In 1871 the multitude of bills in Parliament seeking to permit railroad amalgamations resulted in the appointment of a Commission in 1871 and then of a permanent Railway and Canal Commission in 1873. Its function was to exercise state control over monopolistic enterprises by restricting profits. Monthly conferences to adjust matters relating to competitive rates and traffic in each district "came into existence between 1873 and 1881, and may be said to have closed the period of unrestrained competition."[17] In 1869 the Government purchased all telegraph lines, establishing a monopoly of the telegraph services within the United Kingdom. This was not socialism, but such activity went beyond the boundaries of much liberal thinking, representing a constructive, as contrasted with the more destructive, kind of individual liberalism.

Events abroad, as well as domestic affairs, were working to disturb certain old assumptions of liberal thought. During the first half of the century the guiding political concept of the self-governing national state as the proper and just form of political organization had appeared to be without internal contradictions. The "ripe fruit" theory of empire and the "Little England" conception were the logical consequences of the concept of self-governing nationalism. The Continental revolutionaries of '48 paid more than lip service to the cause; they suffered defeat after defeat because they refused to compromise on the principle. In the unification of Italy in the fifties, appearances were at least in part preserved by the plebiscites. But though the creation of the German Empire by Prussia was to be exalted by many Germans of the Empire as a triumph of the principle of liberal nationalism, inner contradictions had appeared in this realization of the concept, contradictions immediately reflected in the split of the Liberal party in Prussia. For the new Germany was not a self-governing, national state according to the prescribed pattern; it was a dynastic empire composed of a heterogeneous population, including many who were not Germans and who were vociferously unwilling to become citizens of Germany, particularly of a Prussianized Germany; and in vital matters the new Germany was not self-governing. Despite the surface appearance of liberalism conferred by the provision of a constitution and universal manhood suffrage for Reichstag elections, the founding of the German empire was an unpleasant reminder to Liberals elsewhere that the national state might be less important as a just means of organizing the political life of a people than as a more efficient means of organizing the power of any state whatever.

There was nothing new in this. From the time of the American and French Revolutions, and particularly after the enormous success of the French armies in Europe, it had been apparent: what else had led to the Prussian reforms of the Napoleonic era? After Waterloo, the lesson was not forgotten by conservatives: the Holy Alliance was their answer. Only by abolishing the possibility of the national state could the old order survive in a power conflict. But whereas it was remembered as a sort of bad dream by the conservatives, the liberals either never recognized it or forgot it. For them the power of the national state was, except for purposes of defense, irrelevant, since to dream of imperialist conquests made by a self-governing people amounted to a contradiction in terms. Insofar as Continental liberals took their lead from England, they, too, were cosmopolitan and pacifist; insofar as they took it from their own philosophers, they relied either on the inevitable *Zeitgeist*, working through the people, or upon the liberals of other nations. Cavour and Bismarck had not ignored the *Zeitgeist*, but they had added to their calculations the strength of the big battalions.

Other events also awakened renewed concern with the power interests of the state and undermined confidence in other tenets of the liberal creed. The Crimean War had aroused the patriotic passions and national pride of Englishmen, so long restrained. The Civil War in the United States was peculiarly upsetting to those who, like Richard Cobden, believed in a federation of states as the cure for war. The Indian Mutiny and the subsequent assumption of full responsibility by Government for India brought into new prominence the fact that the self-governing state of Great Britain actually ruled as despot, however amiable and well-intentioned, an enormous body of people who could hardly be described as savages. By the late sixties, when Charles Dilke was making his journey around "Greater Britain," the great English-speaking colonies were seeking to erect tariff walls against British, as well as other nations' goods, a strange and troubling indication that self-government would not result in the adoption of liberal economic policies.

But it required the astonishing display of Prussian power between 1866 and 1871 and the threat of German commercial rivalry to awaken Englishmen to the facts of modern power and to lead them to consider seriously their position as one unit in a world of others; to become conscious of themselves as a precariously isolated, variously divided society in which collective interests might be of more serious importance than individual interests. Only as their insular preoccupation waned and as they were faced with industrial and commercial competition did they cease to concentrate so exclusively upon individual, local achievements, and to look at such private enterprises in the light of their possible contribution to the welfare and safety of their whole society.

Once viewed from a national, and yet more from an imperial, perspective, British institutions presented in the third quarter of the century an appearance of kaleidoscopic confusion. The "English chaos," as Huxley and many another described it, was the result of innumerable local, voluntary undertakings. Belief in voluntary action by individuals, the tradition of local responsibility, and fear of control by the central government had conspired to create an almost incredible variety of institutions. When a need was felt, an individual set out to meet it in his own way with such local assistance as he could find. The result was that each institution had its own peculiar organization, each pursued its particular ends in its own way with little, if any, association with similar institutions elsewhere in the country, and each was prepared to guard jealously its autonomy against direction or guidance from without. Inevitably, short of the appearance of a serious crisis, to bring any sort of order out of this confusion would require long and difficult years of effort. Because the years 1866-1871 created something in the nature of a crisis some genuine progress towards re-integration was made in the following two decades. This re-integration movement gained in force throughout the remainder of the century. Already by the eighties Herbert Spencer was declaring that the Liberals, having destroyed the old forms of control, would now have to fight against the new forms of control being created by Parliament.[18] At the same time the economist W. Stanley Jevons was noting that "the most difficult questions arise, not from the relations of the State to individuals, but from its relations to aggregates and organisations of individuals." He drew also the obvious conclusion: "It is impossible that we can have the constant multiplication of institutions and instruments of civilization which evolution is producing, without a growing complication of relations, and a consequent growth of social regulations."[19] The result of the increasing institutional complexity would be necessarily an extension of the supervisory, if not controlling, activity of central governments in the interest of domestic order and national security. Having overthrown the dynastic, aristocratic institutional forms, the industrial and laboring classes now sought to create their own forms of institutional controls in competition with each other.

Much of this was in England clearly independent of any particular influence from foreign sources. But this tendency, inherent, as it were, in the very structure of the developing society, ran counter to the English practices of over a century and to the political prejudices of most Englishmen, whether Liberals or Conservatives. The Liberals had long been fighting, as Spencer noted, against any form of restrictive institutions, public or private, against professionalization (which is institutionalization) against the ordering of affairs, whether by church, state, or corporations of employers or employees. On the other side, the Conservatives, attached to the old institutions which had protected their own interests, found little to admire in the new institutions where privilege depended upon knowledge, talent, or popular approval. Despite these predilections, however, many Englishmen recognized the direction in which their society seemed to be moving. They saw also that the Germans were particularly well prepared to advance in that very direction, as if the *Zeitgeist*, that peculiarly German conception, rewarded its own creators. This accounts for the resistance of most Englishmen to the German influence: that influence was at once alien and repugnant. But it accounts even more definitely for the great influence Germany nevertheless did exert.

The tremendous industrial and commercial advances made by Germany between 1850 and 1885, followed by their tariffs, their colonial pretensions, and diplomatic manoeuvers, were so many warnings that Germany constituted a possible competitor to Britain's leadership, wealth, and power. The periods of near hysteria about the German trade competition, occurring in Britain at intervals after 1880, had a firm foundation in relative growth-rates, however momentarily exaggerated. Meanwhile, if society was to be centrally supervised and bureaucratically organized in the future, whether in the interests of progress or power, to whom might one better turn for lessons and example than to "our Teutonic cousins," as they were now frequently called? In many important respects the shape of the future could be better observed in Germany in the late nineteenth century than in Britain.[20] Many in Britain saw this and, seeking to meet the varied problems presented to Great Britain, turned to the German model.

The influence of the Germans might have been less in the seventies and eighties, however, had not the empirical liberal creed attained and passed its zenith. In the seventies George Eliot was hoping for a Conservative administration to provide a period of stability.[21] This may have been partly due to her age, but her hope reflected a wide feeling among followers of the liberals outside the political party. Similarly Walter Bagehot believed that all the aims of Liberalism which the country would accept had been realized and that a period of consolidation under Conservative leadership was likely.[22] The split of the Liberal party over Home Rule was foreshadowed as well in Joseph Chamberlain's "Unauthorized Program." As the former indicated the rise of a new imperialism among Liberals, the latter voiced demands for greater governmental control over the social conditions in England. The old Liberals, represented in their most extreme positions by John Bright or Herbert Spencer, were bankrupt in the face of the new condition of affairs in the world. They had no program by which to meet the "condition of England" question; they had no program which had not already been tried to meet the new competitive conditions in the world abroad. The Conservatives at least represented a government more likely to follow a national policy of consolidation both at home and abroad.

Those who turned to the Germans for example or model did so, as we shall see, for a great variety of reasons. But they were alike in this: they believed in reform in the national interest, conceiving of the nation as the State, a corporate organization which necessarily exercised a strong, directive influence upon all citizens. All deplored the social "atomism," the "English chaos," and the insular indifference to the world about them. Many wholeheartedly admired the Germans; others feared them and were determined to meet the challenge the rise of Germany promised. Whether in education, in the sciences, in social reform, or in the international arenas of trade and diplomacy, the German influence, long hidden and scorned, became inescapable and triumphant.

Notes

CHAPTER I

1. John Emerich Edward Dahlberg Acton, First Baron Acton, *Historical Studies*, ed. J. N. Figgis and R. V. Laurence (London, 1907), p. 370.

2. John Theodore Merz, *A History of European Thought in the Nineteenth Century* (Edinburgh and London, 1904), I, pp. 160–161, and 167.

3. A. and N. L. Clow, *The Chemical Revolution* (London, 1952), offer such evidence as they could find of the influence of Black and others upon the early developments in chemical industry.

4. Alfred North Whitehead, *Science and the Modern World* (New York, 1926), p. 120.

5. Robert C. Binkley states this well in the first chapter of *Realism and Nationalism, 1852–1871* (New York, 1934), Vol. XVI in *The Rise of Modern Europe*, ed. William L. Langer. Cf. Merz, *op. cit.*, I, 91 ff.

6. The conscious realization of this can be seen in the thought of Werner von Siemens. See his *Personal Recollections*, tr. W. C. Coupland (New York, 1893), pp. 43–46. An early technological entrepreneur, Siemens was the founder of the great electrical firm of Siemens and Halske.

7. Whitehead, *op. cit.*, p. 122; Merz, *op. cit.*, I, 180 ff.

8. See Walter L. Dorn, *Competition for Empire, 1740–1763* (New York, 1940), Vol. IX in *The Rise of Modern Europe* series.

9. See Friederick Paulsen, *German Education, Past and Present* (London, 1908), *passim*.

10. Dorn, *op. cit.*, p. 21.

11. *Ibid.* See also in Robert K. Merton, Ailsa P. Gray, Barbara Hockey, Hanan C. Selvin, eds., *Reader in Bureaucracy* (Glencoe, Ill., 1952), the following: Max Weber, "The Essentials of Bureaucratic Organization," pp. 18–27; Karl Mannheim, "Orientations of Bureaucratic Thought," p. 360; and Robert K. Merton, "Bureaucratic Structure and Personality," pp. 361–377.

12. In addition to Paulsen, see Johannes Conrad, *The German Universities for the Last Fifty Years*, tr. John Hutchinson (Glasgow, 1885). On the school system generally, see I. L. Kandel, "Germany," in *Comparative Education* Peter Sandiford, ed., (London and New York, 1928). In *Education and Society in Modern Germany* (London, 1949), p. 4, R. H. Samuel and R. Hinton Thomas note the continuance of bureaucratic control in Prussia and its influence throughout the empire after 1871.

13. See R. B. Haldane, "Great Britain and Germany," *Universities and National Life* (London, 1912), p. 33.

14. James Hutchison Stirling, *The Secret of Hegel* (London, 1865), II, "Conclusion," esp. p. 533.

15. Beatrice Webb, *My Apprenticeship* (London, 1926), p. 41.

16. James Louis Garvin, *Life of Joseph Chamberlain* (London, 1932), I, p. 188, quoting from John Thackray Bunce, *History of the Corporation of Birmingham* (1885).

17. Thomas C. Williams, *Main Currents of Social and Industrial Change* (London, 1925), p. 63.

18. See Herbert Spencer, *The Man versus the State* (London, 1884).

19. See W. Stanley Jevons, *The State in Relation to Labour*, ed. by Michael Cababé (London, 1894), from first edition of 1882, pp. 31 and 15.

20. See George Malcolm Young, *Victorian England, Portrait of an Age* (London, 1936), p. 256.

21. John Walter Cross, *George Eliot's Life as related in her Letters and Journals* (New York, 1885), III, p. 143.

22. Walter Bagehot, "The Chances for a Long Conservative Regime in England," in *Works*, VII, pp. 82–89.

Chapter II

Professionalization of the Humanistic Studies

The trek of English students to Germany, beginning in the thirties, became an ever-enlarging stream decade by decade until nearly the end of the century. During the fifties and sixties Max Müller, Benjamin Jowett, and Mark Pattison at Oxford were especially active in supporting this trend. In the summer of 1862 James Bryce went to Heidelberg to study law, accompanied by Aeneas Mackay and Henry Nettleship. There they encountered two other groups of students, one led by Albert Venn Dicey and the other by Thomas Hill Green. "Our society is a little Oxford transplanted to Germany," Dicey wrote. When Ingram Bywater went to Bonn in 1868 he carried an introduction from Pattison to Professor Jacob Bernays, as Henry Nettleship did to Professor Emil Hübner.[1] Except for Henry Sidgwick, a member of one of the groups mentioned, these were Oxford men. Cambridge also sent its share of students, but the larger number going from there to Germany were students of the natural or physical sciences.

English students attended the German universities for the same reason that students from all nations went there throughout the century: because the German universities had developed specialized study beyond anything comparable elsewhere. At Oxford and Cambridge serious post-graduate study did not receive institutional recognition, other than through prize essays or examinations for a few fellowships. Through the German-trained students, many of whom returned to teaching careers, German philosophy and German concepts infiltrated and remolded the humanistic studies not only in the two ancient universities, but throughout the United Kingdom.

For English students to be influenced by German thought, however, did not require their studying in German universities nor under German professors in England, nor even a visit to Germany. The most frequent transmission of influence came through books, especially as study of the German language increased and more German books were translated.[2]

A significant change occurred in the study of the classics as a result of the German influence. Specialized study directed attention away from the content of the literature to the history of the language in its formal aspects. Efforts to bring the work in classics at Cambridge and Oxford into line with that of the German universities was undertaken by men who had studied under Germans or otherwise learned from them: by Ingram Bywater, Henry Nettleship, R. D. Hicks, John Peile, and D. B. Munro, among others.[3] Evidence of the new approach to classical studies appeared in the founding of the Oxford Philological Society in 1870, the Cambridge Philological Society in 1871, the Society for the Promotion of Hellenic Studies in 1879, and the British School at Athens in 1885.[4] Under the influence of German scholarship, all studies involving language tended to become philological studies. Students of the classics became classical philologists, and by the eighties anyone who "lapsed into translation"—the phrase is Ingram Bywater's for Jowett—lost caste among the scholars almost as fatally as had Newman a generation earlier by his "lapse and fall"—Gladstone's phrase—into Catholicism.

Central to what was called "scientific scholarship" in the nineteenth century was the historical and comparative philology developed by the Germans. Developed in relation to the idealist and romantic conception of the *Volksgeist*, and furnishing a key to its evolutionary development, this philology and its methods served as the model scientific discipline in the humanistic studies, a position won by its great triumph in establishing the Indo-European line of descent of the Western tongues. As the basis of language study, historical comparative philology stimulated and determined the methods of study for the Oriental languages, archaeology, ethnology, biblical criticism, the classical and modern languages and literatures, and ancient and modern history.[5] The story of its development is therefore of great significance in forming the basis of the *Geisteswissenschaften* or humanistic "sciences" in the nineteenth century.

1.

Triumph of the German comparative historical method in philology and linguistics

Although intercourse between the Occident and the Orient had long been developing, the late eighteenth and early nineteenth centuries covered a period of greatly expanded European interest in all the far corners of the world and of the East particularly. Men of all types, driven by a diversity of impulses, streamed from the West in endless numbers in every direction. Stimulated by the romantic love of the exotic, by a restless quest for adventure and wealth, by missionary interest, and by scientific curiosity, book after book of travels, reflecting the customs, describing the manners, the religions, and other aspects pertaining to alien cultures, flooded European markets. By the middle years of the century, artifacts of the alien cultures, especially of the Near and Far East, but also of Africa and the South Seas, were being transferred to the West: manuscripts, paintings, sculptures, costumes, weapons, household utensils, even the flora and fauna of those distant lands were brought to the West by the shipload. Not only were the maps of the world being rapidly completed, but the cultural knowledge of the world was being extended beyond any limits previously imagined. The founding of museums of all kinds was one of the marked features of the middle decades of the century as the curio cabinets of the eighteenth century gave place to larger collections and more sophisticated classifications. Even before Darwin these were being arranged in evolutionary arrays, according to subject classifications, as by Lane-Fox Pitt-Rivers in his collection of fire-arms.[6] Only those cultural groups with a pretense of being part of the European community, such as Italy and Greece, were able in the nineteenth century to resist the acquisitive drive of the collectors.

However imperialistic a procedure, the traffic was by no means one-way, nor was it restricted to the more tangible forms of merchandise. Though the imperialist story is often told as if it were only an imposition of the West upon others, importations affect the importers, and often in unexpected ways. One of the important importations, which was scarcely regarded as an important commodity by the commercial operators, was that of the languages and philosophies of the East. The mystical, transcendental philosophies and theologies of the East proved particularly attractive to the romantics and idealists, and an ever-enlarging reading public became acquainted with a great body of literature of distinctly different cultural traditions. This was possible only after a knowledge of Eastern tongues and a systematic cultivation of that knowledge had been acquired. And, as in so many other instances, this study, too, was begun by Englishmen and Frenchmen, but ultimately was much more systematically carried on by Central Europeans, especially by the Germans.

As a direct result of the English and French occupation of India, Englishmen and Frenchmen began the study of Sanskrit, the ancient language of the Hindus, from which the Germans developed the discipline of historical, comparative philology. Among the earliest Englishmen to study Sanskrit were William Jones, Charles Williams, Henry Thomas Colebrooke, and Horace Hayman Wilson.[7] All began their studies in the service of the East India Company and all became masters of the language. Only Wilson ever occupied a university post. In 1832 he was appointed to the newly-founded Boden Professorship in Sanskrit at Oxford. Upon succeeding Williams as librarian to East India House, however, he removed to London in 1836, thereafter visiting Oxford only for a part of each term.[8] As a consequence, none of these English scholars trained successors or disciples to develop such insights as Jones had acquired as early as 1786 when he wrote that, in relation to Latin and Greek, Sanskrit

> bears a stronger affinity, both in the roots of verbs and in the forms of grammar, than could possibly have been produced by accident; so strong indeed, that no philologer could examine all three without believing them to have sprung from some common source, which, perhaps, no longer exists;

there is a similar reason, though not quite so forcible, for supposing that both the Gothick and the Celtick, though blended with a very different idiom, had the same origin with the Sanskrit.[9]

The founder of the French school of Sanskrit studies was Anquetil du Perron who enlisted in the French army as a means of getting to India to study that language, but was later relieved of his army duties and assisted financially by the French government. Upon his return to France, he published a three-volume translation of the Zend-Avesta (1771). France became thereafter the continental center of Sanskrit study and it was from Paris, where so many Germans, later to acquire fame, went to study between 1800 and 1830, that the study was exported to Germany.

The brothers, Friedrich and Wilhelm von Schlegel, studied in Paris, beginning in 1803, and Friedrich published in 1808 in Heidelberg *Über die Sprache und Weisheit der Indier*. For the Schlegels the language was a source for the study of Indian culture and its history, as well as for the history of language. In his work, Friedrich adumbrated an insight, much like Jones' earlier, which was to have a profound effect upon philological study: "Comparative grammar will give us entirely new information on the genealogy of languages, in exactly the same way in which comparative anatomy has thrown light upon natural history."[10] The different effects of the two germinative ideas, English and German, was due to the different cultural settings into which they fell: the German did not fall upon institutionally barren ground. Wilhelm von Schlegel became professor of Sanskrit in the University of Bonn and the study of Sanskrit as a discipline for students was established.

But there was an additional reason that the German insight flourished: it was conceived as part of a philosophy which was being developed simultaneously in many branches of study. Contemporary with the Schlegels, Karl Friedrich Eichhorn and Karl von Savigny, both idealists and romanticists, developed the concept of law as an expression of the *Volksgeist*, arising out of custom and popular feeling, "by silently operating forces, not by the arbitrary will of a lawgiver."[11] From this organic developmental theory sprang the concept of the laws of organic evolution, such as that growth proceeds from the simple to the complex, or that ontogeny recapitulates phylogeny, and also the use of the comparative method as a means of demonstrating such laws. The student's first duty was to seek out the most ancient expressions of the *Geist*, since the earliest forms were likely to provide evidence of the character of the germinal archetype out of which all subsequent forms had developed; the student then studied the evolutionary development through changing forms into the more complex. By constantly comparing similar forms for minute differences in complexity, each form could ultimately be assigned its proper place in the long developmental line of emergent growth. Since societies had everywhere developed by similar stages from primitive communal forms to differentiated "higher" forms, represented by the Western European societies, every "expression" of a people, its religion, language, literature, laws, its political and social institutions, could be traced by the comparative method.[12]

When in 1805 von Savigny went to Paris, he was accompanied by Jakob Grimm, who was seeking manuscripts of the old German folk literature, as examples of the regional German literary forms. His comparative grammar of the Germanic languages (1819) made him one of the founders of the comparative study of philology. A precursor, Rasmus K. Rask, from Denmark, was the first to perceive the outlines of an Indo-European "tree" of languages. But it was left to another German scholar, Franz Bopp, who had also studied Sanskrit in Paris and in London, to lay the foundations of the study, initially with a book in 1816 in which he treated the verbal inflection of Sanskrit in comparison with the Greek, Latin, Persian, and Germanic languages.

In the thirties, a student of F. W. J. von Schelling, who had studied Sanskrit with Hermann Brockhaus at Leipzig and with Bopp at Berlin, adopted as his life-work the translation of the *Rigveda*. This was F. Max Müller who, after working with Eugène Burnouf in Paris, went to England in the late forties to seek financial assistance from the East India Company.[13] The Chevalier Bunsen, then Prussian Ambassador, was immediately attracted to him and introduced him to the leading Germanists in England. A place was found for him at Oxford where, though later defeated for the chair in Sanskrit by Charles Williams—a direct expression of anti-German feeling by the conservative Churchmen[14]—he was made the first Taylorian professor of modern European languages. A brilliant lecturer, Müller remained at Oxford for over fifty years, becoming one of the important luminaries of the university. Throughout his life, though married to an English woman and residing in England, Müller remained strongly German in his sympathies and, like many of the German chemists, in the early seventies seriously contemplated returning to the Fatherland, and for much the same reason: English indifference to scholarship and research.[15]

His lectures in the fifties and sixties diffused some knowledge of the German philological studies throughout the University and resulted in the creation for him of a chair in Comparative Philology. One of his students was E. B. Cowell, who became professor of Sanskrit at Cambridge in 1867; another was A. H. Sayce, tutor at Oxford, long Müller's deputy, and subsequently professor of Assyriology.[16] Sayce had also studied under John Rhys, professor of Celtic at Oxford, who had studied linguistics at Leipzig. Through Müller, Joseph Wright, who studied at Heidelberg and Leipzig, was introduced to Oxford in 1882.[17]

At Cambridge the comparative philology of the Germans was introduced into the classical studies by John William Donaldson, whose *New Cratylus* (1839) won Thomas Arnold's praise.[18] Among Donaldson's students was John Peile who went to Göttingen to study Sanskrit. From Peile's lectures on Sanskrit and comparative philology at Christ's Church, Skeat dated the introduction of the latter discipline at Cambridge.[19]

Joseph Bosworth of Oxford published a grammar and a dictionary in Anglo-Saxon (1838) which showed some acquaintance with Rask and Grimm.[20] The genuine importers of the new methods in this subject, however, were J. M. Kemble and Benjamin Thorpe. The latter had studied with Rask in Copenhagen. Kemble was a Cambridge man of the group of Apostles who, after taking only a poll degree, went to Germany in 1829. At Munich he read Kant, but it was the study of Teutonic philology with Jakob Grimm at the University of Berlin which determined the direction of his work.[21] Returning to England, he worked in the Cambridge libraries from 1832 to 1835. In that last year he became editor of the *British and Foreign Review*, a kind of predecessor of the later *Academy*, and one of the few English journals distinguished for an interest in scholarly work done on the continent. Between them, Kemble and Thorpe edited and interpreted almost all the important works of Anglo-Saxon poetry, making it possible "for a race of scholars to arise who were not compelled to go abroad to learn the philology of their native tongue."[22]

English literature was not taught except in the Scottish universities and in the two London university colleges. And even in Scotland, the teaching in this subject was associated primarily with logic and rhetoric until the advent of David Masson, trained at University College, London.[23] In England the study of English literature was dominated by amateurs. Such an indefatigable worker and promoter of scholarly societies for the advancement of English literature as F. J. Furnival was only by chance, as it were, a University man and he never held an academic post. Even Walter William Skeat had studied Anglo-Saxon at King's College School before entering Cambridge and he prepared there for a clerical career. When a throat disorder closed a position in the Church to him, he returned to Christ's Church in 1864—as a lecturer in mathematics. His appointment to the chair of Anglo-Saxon in 1878 may be taken as the date of the founding of professional scholarship in English language and literature at Cambridge.[24] Despite his efforts to encourage the study of English literature, however, when a tripos was established in medieval and modern languages in 1885, it was given the inevitable philological cast by the importation of two German philologists, Karl Breul and E. G. W. Braunholtz, who lacked any interest in imaginative literature except as a source of problems in language. Becoming the first professor of German and a reader in Romance languages respectively, the two determined "the nature of modern language, including English, study at Cambridge."[25]

At Oxford modern languages were taught only at the Taylorian Institution where students were few and the teaching was on an elementary level. When the chair of comparative philology was founded for Max Müller, the chair in modern languages was abolished.[26] Scholarship was represented by Dr. Heinrich Krebs from the University of Freiburg, a scholar in German and sub-librarian at the Taylorian;[27] and, outside the Taylorian, by Dr. Adolf Neubauer, a Hebrew scholar, from the Universities of Prague and Munich, sub-librarian at the Bodleian. When finally a chair was founded in English language and literature in 1885, to make it academically acceptable and not simply a dilettante course, such as historians William Stubbs and Edward A. Freeman feared, the philological aspect had again to be the major interest. Hence a German-trained philologist, Arthur Sampson Napier, whose personal taste in literature ran exclusively to detective stories, received the appointment.[28]

After 1850, students of language and literature returning from German universities brought with them this "scientific" philological interest. An erudite discipline, requiring exacting work, its mastery gave entrance to the arcana of professional knowledge and served to distinguish the professional scholar from the amateur and journalist. In Britain this was almost wholly the result of the German influence.

2.

Influence upon history, religion, jurisprudence, anthropology, and geography

The close relationship between philological studies and the study of history can hardly be over-emphasized. The very purpose of philology as first envisioned was to lay a solid foundation for the study of *Kulturgeschichte* and many early nineteenth century historians from Leopold Ranke in Germany to Kemble in England began their studies in philology, just as it was from the philologists that the seminar method of instruction was adopted by the German historians. Kemble laid the foundations for the scholarly study of English history. His most important work, *The Saxons in England* (1849), established for over a generation the "germ theory" of the Teutonic mark as the source of the English tradition of representative government.[29] For William Stubbs, he was "my pattern scholar,"[30] no mean praise, while F. W. Maitland, a severer critic, observed that "Kemble's work often requires correction; but if Kemble's work had not been there, there would have been nothing to correct."[31]

The earlier historians of England, writers such as Francis Palgrave, Sharon Turner, Henry Hallam and John Lingard, and even Thomas Babington Macaulay, though well-acquainted with the sources, were, strictly speaking, amateurs, and founded no schools. Maitland wrote of Palgrave that he would have been a great commander if an army had been forthcoming. "We had our swallows, and beautiful birds they were; but there was spring in Germany."[32] The army was not forthcoming because Palgrave and the others had no opportunity to enlist men under their banners; none held university posts, and with the state of the universities in the pre-reform years such posts would probably have availed them little.

William Stubbs had been an Anglo-Saxon scholar before he entered Oxford, having learned the language and made use of it for historical purposes in a commercial academy where, in addition to the classics, he also studied French and German.[33] After graduating from Christ Church, Oxford in 1848, he began, as he was to end, his career in the Church. Following his early publications and appointment as editor of the Rolls series, he was made Regius Professor of Modern History at Oxford in 1866.

Like other professors, Stubbs found few pupils because "nearly all study in Oxford is directed towards the securing of honours in the Class Lists," and though an honours school of modern history and law had been founded, students depended, as in other studies, upon the college tutors.[34] The character of the instruction for the examinations in the history school can be imagined from the fact that Mandell Creighton was able to tutor in modern history, though he "had had only six months' study of modern history before he was called upon to teach it."[35]

Stubbs introduced himself to Oxford "as a worker in history" and through his influence on the tutors and a few students, one may say with Creighton that with him "began the scientific pursuit of history" at Oxford. Though Stubbs was to write of "our comparative method," he did not introduce any training in scholarly method or research.[36] As one of his students, T. F. Tout, wrote many years later: "The truth is that all of us of the older generation have had to pick up our historical method by accident and rule of thumb."[37] Even the Modern History Society, later to become the Stubbs' Society, of which as professor he became the first president, was founded by an American student, Brearley, (who missed at Oxford the seminars of the German universities.[38]) In 1876, after comparing the prize essays written at Oxford with the doctoral essays of the Germans, to the great disadvantage of the former, Stubbs added: "We are . . . but at the beginning of our work; we have very much to do still before the History School of Oxford can take its stand beside the historical schools of Paris or Bonn, or Goettingen, or Munich, or Vienna . . ."[39] Nor, apart from his own writing, did he do anything to advance that work in the few remaining years of his professorship.[40]

Stubbs was thoroughly acquainted with the works of Waitz and Gneist, the Maurers, Brunner, and Sohm; he admitted the pre-eminence of the Germans even in the history of England.[41] Though the Germanism of his own work was carefully guarded, no one more thoroughly believed that "the history of Germany is bound up with our national and natural identity."[42] Edward Freeman, his successor at Oxford, also followed the Teutonic lead; in America he lectured on "Old England, Middle England, and New England." By "Old England" he meant Schleswick or Germany![43]

At Cambridge, a history tripos was established in 1873 during the professorship of J. R. Seeley, who slanted the examination toward his own interest in politics and the training of statesmen. Seeley was deeply influenced by Ranke's view of the State and was intimately acquainted with German work as his *Life of Stein* attests.[44] To call him, as Mrs. Creighton did, a literary man is probably not fair; like most of the scholars of his day, his interests were varied. His "conversation class" was the nearest approach to a seminar class in history in either of the two great universities.[45] Nevertheless a professional approach to history at Cambridge may be said to have awaited the coming of Mandell Creighton as professor of ecclesiastical history in 1884. Creighton addressed his inaugural to the theologians, he said, because he found them, in contrast to the historians, "strong in the use of the historical method." Soon he was able to revise the history examination to give it a more historical orientation.[46]

An indication of the rise of interest in professional history was the founding of the *English Historical Review* in 1886. The

founders were Lord Acton, James Bryce, R. W. Church, Mandell
Creighton, York Powell, and A. W. Ward.[47] Creighton, who found
all English histories "insular" and only those written by Germans
of any worth,[48] became the first editor with Reginald Poole,
Stubb's student, with a a doctorate from Leipzig, as his assistant
and successor.[49] It was fitting that the lead article in the first number was an essay on German historians by Lord Acton, who was
himself educated at the University of Munich, and was "never
more than half an Englishman."[50]

Barthold Niebuhr was the first great exemplar in the professional
study of ancient history. Through the early liberal Anglicans and
especially through Arnold, he influenced historical thought at the
two universities. He exercised also a strong influence upon George
Grote, who attributed the superiority of Thirlwall's and his own
histories to the fact that "philological studies have been prosecuted
in Germany with remarkable success."[51] Grote's *History of Greece*
and Mommsen's work on Roman history were reported as effect-
ing "a revolution" in the English universities.[52]

Max Müller's influence, important as it was in philology, was
perhaps even greater outside the University in the study of comparative mythology and comparative religions. In addition to
editing the long series of volumes entitled *The Wisdom of the
East*, initiated in 1875, which provided English readers with their
first large body of materials on Eastern faiths, he lectured widely
on the subject.[53] So sympathetic was he to all religious approaches,
so closely did he approach an entirely non-creedal position, that
throughout his life he was subject to the serious accusation of being
a pantheist.[54]

Against Müller's own continual protestations of his Christian
faith may be placed for contrast Beatrice Webb's testimony concerning the effect of studying these alien religions. She has recorded
how, during the mid-seventies, the years of Max Müller's greatest
popularity in England:

> . . . intellectual curiosity swept me into currents of thought
> at that time stirring the minds of those who frequented the
> . . . more cultivated circles of London society; movements
> which though unconnected with, and in some ways con-
> tradictory to each other had the common characteristic of

undermining belief in traditional Christianity. The most immediately subversive of these ferments, because it seemed to provide an alternative form of religious emotion, arose out of the opening up of the religions of the Far East . . . And yet Buddhism and Hinduism found in me no convert. All that happened was my detachment from Christianity."[55]

The difference in the effect of the study of comparative religions upon the young English woman and the German perhaps depended as much upon their backgrounds as upon anything else. Müller's metaphysics assumed that dialectical relations existed within an essential unity, that there is an essential oneness of things in any final view, however conflicting might be the manifestations arising from the separateness involved in their phenomenal appearance. For him, these contrasts and differences did not annul each other; they were dialectical appearances assumed by the universal *Geist*.

Even though his religious faith might be broad enough to include all religions within an ideal whole, in practical affairs, in matters political, Müller could be coldly realistic. The attractive serenity of many Germans, especially among the scholars and scientists of the first half of the nineteenth century, the universal breadth of their interests, their deep sympathies with alien cultures was not incompatible with an almost conscienceless nationalism, particularly as the realization of a German national state appeared to them to be peculiarly decreed by the *Zeitgeist*. No one could have been more pleased than Max Müller with the events in Germany from 1866-1871. In 1866 he confided in a letter to his mother that "The methods employed might have been better, here and there, but Prussia staked her existence to make Germany united and strong, and . . . I rejoice over the results. Prussia will have a yet harder war to wage, for war with France can hardly be avoided . . . but in the Protestant North an independent power must be created, be it called Prussia or Germany . . ."[56] This was a realistic reading of the future. To Edward Freeman, strongly pro-German, he wrote in August, 1870: "Peace will be easy, for Germany wants no conquests, not even Alsace and Lorraine . . ." Having learned better, he was two months later defending their annexation to Gladstone: "Were Prussia to yield Strassburg and Alsace, Prussia would cease to be Prussia." In a letter to Dr.

Abeken, Bismarck's secretary during the war, Max Müller suggested Machiavellian tactics to placate the English liberals: "There are in England also some voices in favour of a *plébiscite* in the parts to be annexed. To me it seems an un-German comedy, which however might be acted in Alsace with good prospect of success, 'by desire'. "[57] Here spoke not only a patriot but a realist in politics.

This political realism followed from a paternalistic conception of man and society and from the acceptance of a theoretical ideal goal for the State, in the attainment of which any means is acceptable. Men in general require leadership and direction which is the responsibility of the aristocratic and the expert to provide. They must be controlled and directed with a view less to their immediately desired ends than to the ultimate ends of the State in order that the potentiality of the national *Geist* may be realized.

That such a paternalistic conception should also appeal to English conservatives was foreordained: it was their own. That it should arise also from the experience of Englishmen governing India or prove acceptable to them was almost equally inevitable. Again the influence of the Germans and the East coincided: German idealism with the practical realities of imperial rule.

That the experience of governing India had a tendency to produce politically conservative thinking was the belief of Bentham, James Mill, and liberals like Cobden, George Cornewall Lewis, and Goldwin Smith.[58] The correctness of the belief seemed to be illustrated in the life of James Fitzjames Stephen. A Benthamite liberal and circuit-riding attorney, he went to India in 1868 as law member of the viceroy's commission. On his return voyage to England in 1872, he began the composition of *Liberty, Equality, Fraternity*, an attack on the social and political philosophy of John Stuart Mill, or what its author described as "virtually a consideration of the commonplace of British politics in the light of his Indian experience."[59] From Thomas Hobbes, Stephen adopted a belief in the necessity of force to maintain order in a society. "Force," he contended, "is always in the background, and the invisible bond which corresponds to the moral framework of society."[60] Certainly this was true in respect to the government of India by the British *raj*, though hardly to be described as invisible there. If Stephen seems to have had a constitutional predilection for such a view, it was re-enforced and confirmed by his Indian sojourn.

Even after his return from India, however, he stood for election as a Liberal candidate.[61] Defeated, he recognized that he was less averse to the Conservative position than he had believed earlier. In Carlyle, that great wet-nurse of imperialists, with whom he enjoyed Sunday afternoon walks, he found much that proved congenial: attacks on parliamentary government, representative institutions, and democratic notions. In the eighties Stephen was a full-fledged imperialist.

Stephen's progress from Benthamite liberalism to Conservative imperialism was not an isolated instance of such a course. Nor was it only the Indian experience which had a tendency to promote Conservative thinking. Of John Austin, who traversed a similar path, John Stuart Mill recorded:

> . . . Like me, he never ceased to be an utilitarian, and with all his love of the Germans, and enjoyment of their literature, never became in the smallest degree reconciled to the innate-principle of metaphysics. He cultivated more and more a kind of German religion . . . while in politics . . . he acquired an indifference, bordering on contempt, for the progress of popular institutions; though he rejoiced in that of Socialism, as the most effectual means of compelling the powerful classes to educate the people . . . He professed great disrespect for what he called 'the universal principles of human nature of the political economists,' . . . the modes of thinking of his later years, and especially of his last publication, were much more Tory in their general character than those which he held at this time.[62]

Few passages more revelatory of the effect of the early German influence upon those who were not Churchmen, even to the distrust of German metaphysics, can be found: the utilitarian liberal who, under that influence, in educating the people, becomes sympathetic to socialism, acquires an indifference to popular institutions, distrusts the view of the nature of man underlying the classical political economy, and winds up a political conservative.

The confluence of these two influences, the German and imperial, often difficult to separate in subsequent conservative political thought, appeared in the work of Henry Maine. Founder of the Oxford school of historical jurisprudence, Maine was "Savigny's disciple," the German historical school of law providing the "source of inspiration for his philosophy of history."[63] As with his German mentors, Maine's method was also suggested by historical, comparative philology: "if the materials for this process are sufficient, and if the comparisons be accurately executed," he wrote of his work, "the methods followed are as little objectionable as those which have led to such surprising results in comparative philology."[64] Reflecting the German developmental theories,[65] Maine found collectivism characteristic of primitive societies and he posited a progressive evolution from status to contract characteristic of the advancement of human society, a more sophisticated version of Spencer's law of development from the homogeneous to the heterogeneous derived from a similar source. His *Ancient Law,* published two years after Darwin's *Origin of Species,* exhibited no Darwinian influence, though in later work the author utilized Darwinian arguments.

But Maine's experience in India had also a formative effect upon his thought; his experience as law member of the Governor General's Council in India united with the German influence to produce the Conservative theorist. "If there were an ideal Toryism I should probably be a Tory," he wrote. "The truth is, India and the Indian Office make one judge public men by standards which have little to do with public opinion."[66] What the result of such judgment might be appeared in his work on *Popular Government* in 1885.

Maine's reading of human nature was that of the usual conservative despair, modified by his experience of the Indian reluctance to accept a British-dictated British way of life. Unlike the learned and aristocratic, most men, he argued, are ignorant, unintelligent, slaves to custom, given to disorder. Democratic government will oppose progressive change; it is, as history has shown, unable to endure long; it is inefficient and unable to meet the increasingly complex problems of modern, progressive societies. Avoiding Comte's solution of turning government over to scientific experts, Maine would retain the aristocracy in power, for it was they who had been responsible for the gradual progress made by modern European societies.

Like the Liberal Anglicans, Maine owed his conception of evolutionary progress to the Germans, but what assured him great authority was that, in addition to a judicial manner, his theory permitted even the aristocratic conservatives to embrace the idea of progress. When the Liberals talked of progress, they seemed always to imply the destruction of British institutions or an almost revolutionary amendment: disestablishment of the Church, abolition of the House of Lords, and universal manhood suffrage. But Maine presented the Conservatives with a theory of progress, so necessary in the dynamic new world that was dawning, which had the enormous attraction of placing change either in the past or safely under their own control. Maine represented the conservative accommodation to the doctrine of progress, of individualism even to atomism, and a society based upon contract,—an accommodation with a difference such as was occurring in many other areas during these decades when the industrial and financial magnates associated with them gradually entered the ranks of the Conservatives and so prepared the way for the Whig break with the Liberal party in 1886.

Besides introducing the comparative historical method of the Germans into the study of jurisprudence and setting his disciples the task of tracing out the details of England's legal history, Maine's *Ancient Law* became widely influential outside the academic world. Walter Bagehot not only quoted from it at length in the first chapter of *Physics and Politics*, too often regarded as simply a social Darwinist tract, but his main theses owed as much to Maine as to Darwin: the emphasis upon the weight of custom in society, the resistance of the majority to change, the leadership of an élite in social progress, and the importance of imitation in disseminating social innovations.

James Bryce, Maine's colleague at Oxford, had studied under Vangerow at Heidelberg, and was largely responsible for the development of a school of law at Oxford. When a readership in Roman Law was founded in 1881, "the opportunity [was] taken of placing it in the learning, the energy and zeal of a German civilian—Dr. Grueber."[67] At Cambridge, after 1884, the historical study of law was the province of F. W. Maitland. Though early stimulated by Savigny, it was after reading Brunner and Sohm that Maitland determined to do for English law what the Germans had done for Roman law.[68]

Anthropology at Oxford was indebted to comparative historical philology not only through Maine but also through its first reader (1878), Edward B. Tylor. Educated in a Dissenters' academy, Tylor might well have belonged to an older generation, so much was his work characteristic of that of the English amateur scientists. A Quaker, he was, like many of the scientists of that faith, skeptical of theory. His method was defined by R. R. Marett as that of the dragnet: to gather first and sift afterwards: "in a single chapter of his *Researches* (1865), it would almost seem as if he had thrown his facts together by the handful trusting to no more than a sort of divination . . . that some kind of useful generalization will come out of it somehow."[69] A naive empiricist, Tylor adopted unquestioningly the basic postulate of the associationist psychology; that men's minds work everywhere similarly. The whole tendency of his thought reflected the traditional liberal mind of his day. But in his chosen study, hit upon almost accidentally, he discovered that the Germans had been there before him, particularly the two von Humboldts, Klemm, Waitz, Bastian, and Max Müller.[70] From the study of philology, he learned of the comparative method and its historical uses;[71] from the *Kulturgeschichte* of the Germans he took the term "Culture-history as it is conveniently called in Germany," shortening it in his next work to "culture," meaning "the history, not of tribes or nations, but of the condition of knowledge, religion, art, custom, and the like among them."[72]

This anthropological concept of culture, because its application was to "primitives," did not immediately have the effect of relativizing social concepts and social attitudes, as it has since; such cultures remained firmly fixed in their historical niche while the contemporary bearers were regarded as laggards in the progressive development of man into civilized societies. Nevertheless, increased knowledge of the varieties of human behavior and social relationships inevitably undermined complete confidence in Western European standards, requiring at least some reconsideration and defense of the accepted conventions. The impact of extra-Europeans, though only beginning, was by the third quarter of the century becoming almost inescapable among the educated classes.

Meanwhile at Cambridge, a young Scottish Fellow of Trinity College, James George Frazer, had been directed towards the study of anthropology by W. Robertson Smith and James Ward[73] who called his attention to Tylor's *Primitive Culture*. Robertson's interest in totemism, early treated by John Ferguson McLennan, influenced Frazer and led him to the great work of his life, *The Golden Bough*. As Frazer himself recognized, this was a direct application of the comparative historical method to the religions of different races and ages.[74]

If Tylor, self-trained, never systematically organized the teaching of his subject, he was, nevertheless, influential through writing and lecturing in forming an English school of professional anthropology. He was also instrumental in bringing about an anthropological section in the British Association in 1884.[75]

As a distinct subject of study, anthropology developed, however, more slowly than geography, perhaps because of the activities of the long-established Royal Geographical Society. This society, composed of a sprinkling of explorers surrounded by amateur enthusiasts, became concerned about the lack of geographical studies in Britain and appointed J. S. Keltie to investigate the situation. He reported in 1885.[76] In keeping with the imperialist thought of the day, Keltie endorsed geographical study by relating it to Europe's cultural mission to the world and its universal interest. "A systematic scientific conception of geography will take the whole earth's surface as the subject of its comparative studies, and all the more when at the present time European culture is pressing forward on every hand with rapid progress." To describe the condition of geographical studies in Britain, he approvingly quoted an anonymous educational authority: "(1) In Universities it is nil. (2) In Public Schools very nearly nil . . . (3) It is required for the Public Services, and taught, I do not know how, by crammers. (4) The only places where geography is systematically taught in England, are the Training Colleges, male and female, and the National Board Schools; with now, and of the last few years, some few good High and Middle-Class Schools."[77] All continental countries had university classes in the subject—twelve in the twenty-one German universities—and by official regulations, prescribed courses in it for all grades of schools. "Germany may be taken as the model which all the other Continental countries are following, as far as their special circumstances will permit."[78]

By the third quarter of the century geography had become a German science as in the eighteenth it had been French. The two founders of modern geography were Alexander von Humboldt, influenced by Kant, and Karl Ritter, influenced by Rousseau, Pestalozzi, and the post-Kantian German idealist philosophers. Ritter viewed the earth as a great organic whole, composed of many subsidiary organic regional units, each with an individual organization. Seeking to define each regional organic whole, Ritter strove also to define the inner relations which teleologically bound the many regional wholes into the great totality. Humboldt, strongly influenced by French scientists, among whom he lived for many years, was, more than Ritter, a devotee of empirical methods of investigation, but he was, no more than Ritter, content to stop with empirical generalities. "In many groups of phenomena," he wrote in *Cosmos*, "we must still content ourselves with the recognition of empirical laws; but the highest and more rarely attained aim of all natural inquiry must ever be the discovery of their *causal connexion*."[79] Both men consciously employed the comparative method and made Berlin, where Ritter taught both in the University and the War Academy, the center of geographical study. According to H. J. Mackinder, the founder of the modern British school of geography, "the Prussian officers of 1866 and 1870 were as truly his [Ritter's] intellectual offspring as was the *Erdkunde* of which Schlegel said that it was the Bible of Geography."[80]

Keltie, in concluding his report, particularly urged the founding of chairs in the universities and in 1887, as a result of prodding from the Royal Geographical Society, the University of Oxford established a readership in the subject. Appointed to the office in 1888, Mackinder not only established the subject at Oxford but encouraged its study throughout the United Kingdom. In 1895, when the International Geographic Congress met in London, he was able to celebrate the occasion as a "memorable year for English students of geography. We have entertained in London for the first time a great gathering of our foreign colleagues, and have presented to the British public the unfamiliar spectacle of a geographical meeting, in which scholars and professors were as prominent as explorers."[81] Noting that Britain had never lacked pioneers in geography and had contributed to precise survey and other parts of the subject, he continued: "It is rather on the synthetic and philosophical, and therefore on the educational, side of our subject that we fall so markedly below the foreign and especially the German standard." Although the situation in Britain was slowly improving, yet the subject "has no appreciable position in degree-examinations; there are no examinations at all for the post of secondary teacher, nor is there anywhere in the land anything really comparable to the German Geographical Institute." English specialists in the subject were "almost invariably compelled to use German maps."[82]

Notes

CHAPTER II

1. *Memorials of Albert Venn Dicey*, ed. Robert S. Rait (London, 1925), p. 36. Others from Oxford included A. O. Rutson, H. G. Dakins, and Donald Crawford, a fellow of Lincoln College; Henry Sidgwick from Cambridge. See also Diderik Roll-Hansen, *The Academy, 1869–1879, Anglistica*, VIII (Copenhagen, 1957), p. 83.

2. Many German immigrants of the '48 group found occupation either in teaching the language or in translating German books. See C. R. Hennings, *Deutsche in England* (Stuttgart, 1923), pp. 67–85.

3. Of these men, Ingram Bywater studied at Bonn and Heidelberg, Henry Nettleship at Berlin, John Peile at Göttingen; Hicks' edition of Aristotle's *Politics* was based on Franz Susemihl's; see the next note for D. B. Monro.

4. Founders of the Cambridge Philological Society were E. B. Cowell, Kennedy, and H. A. J. Munro; W. G. Clark and R. C. Jebb of Trinity; F. A. Paley, J. E. B. Mayor and J. E. Sandys of St. John's; W. W. Skeat and J. Peile of Christ's; and C. A. M. Fennell of Jesus College. *The Academy*, II (1871), p. 211. The active agent in the

founding of the Oxford Philological Society was D. B. Monro who is reported holding "German learning and research in high honour" (J. Cook Wilson, *David Binning Monro* [Oxford, 1907], pp. 10–11.) The Society for the Promotion of Hellenic studies was founded among others by Monro; Charles Newton of the British Museum and University College, London; A. H. Sayce; and Percy Gardner who in 1877 had been "excited in Greece by German excavations at Olympia" (*D. N. B.*). See also the account by Sir Charles Dilke in Stephen Gwynn and Gertrude M. Tuckwell, *Life of the Rt. Hon. Sir Charles Dilke* (London, 1917) I, p. 280. Charles Newton was with Arthur John Evans (Göttingen) also active in the founding of the British School at Athens. In urging the founding of these schools the scholars invariably referred to the French and more particularly the German schools, already long established. See R. C. Jebb, "An English School of Archaeology," *Contemporary Review*, 33 (Aug.-Nov., 1878), pp. 776–789.

5. See for example A. H. Sayce, "The Needs of Historical Science," in *Endowment of Research* (London, 1876), esp. pp. 200–201; and E. B. Cowell *Inaugural Lecture* (London and Cambridge, 1867), esp. p. 6; and Duncan Forbes, *The Liberal Anglican Idea of History* (Cambridge, 1952) pp. 139–142.

6. See A. Lane-Fox Pitt-Rivers, *The Evolution of Culture and Other Essays*, ed. J. L. Myres with an introduction by Henry Balfour (Oxford, 1906), esp. p. v.

7. See Holger Pedersen, *Linguistic Science in the Nineteenth Century*, tr. John Webster Spargo (Cambridge, 1931) on which the following account of the development of comparative philology is largely based.

8. "Wilson, Horace Hayman," *D. N. B.*

9. "Jones, William," *D. N. B.* and Pedersen, *op. cit.*, p. 18.

10. Pedersen, *ibid.* p. 18.

11. Ernest Barker, *Political Thought in England*, Home University Library (London), p. 164.

12. See Forbes, *op. cit.*, pp. 15–16, *et passim*.

13. G. M. Müller, ed., *Life and Letters of Friedrich Max Müller* (London, 1902). On his influence in comparative philology and modern languages in England, see C. A. Firth, *The School of English Language and Literature* (Oxford and London, 1909), pp. 21–22, and the same author's *Modern Languages at Oxford, 1724–1929* (London, 1929), esp. p. 54. See also Klaus Dockhorn, *Der deutsche Historismus in England* (Göttingen and Baltimore, 1950), *passim*.

14. See Evelyn Abbott and Lewis Campbell, *Life and Letters of Benjamin Jowett* (London, 1897) I, p. 291.

15. G. M. Müller, *op. cit.*, I, pp. 514, 529.

16. Cowell had also studied with H. H. Wilson, and Sayce with John Rhys, professor of Celtic, who had studied at Leipzig.

17. Another of Max Müller's students was the phoneticist Henry Sweet who also studied at Heidelberg.

18. The *New Cratylus* (1839) was founded, according to the preface, on the comparative grammar of Bopp. See Forbes, *op. cit.*, p. 138; Dockhorn, *op, cit.*, pp. 57–60.

19. W. W. Skeat, "John Peile," *Proceedings of the British Academy*, IV (1909–10), pp. 378–382. Among his students were Peter Giles, W. H. D. Rouse, and R. Seymour Conway.

20. See R. W. Chambers, *Inaugural Lecture* (London, 1923); and Bruce Dickins, "J. M. Kemble and Old British Scholarship," *Proceedings of the British Academy*, XXV (1939).

21. To Grimm, Kemble dedicated his edition of *Beowulf* in 1833. See Dickins, *op. cit.*, p. 14.

22. R. W. Chambers, *op. cit.* p. 5.

23. See "Skeat, Walter William," *D. N. B.*

24. See Stephen Potter, *The Muse in Chains* (London, 1937), pp. 104 ff.

25. E. M. W. Tillyard, *The Muse Unchained* (London, 1958), p. 29.

26. Potter, *op. cit.*, p. 163; Firth, *op. cit.*, p. 36.

27. *Ibid.*, p. 63.

28. *Ibid.*, p. 24; Potter, *op. cit.*, pp. 183 ff. See also Louis R. Farnell, *An Oxonian Looks Back* (London, 1934), who notes: "I have rarely known an educated man with so little flair for pure literature." Arthur Sampson Napier, an Oxford man, had been *Privat-dozent* in English at the University of Berlin and *Ausserordentlicher* professor at the University of Göttingen.

29. Dickins, *op. cit.*, pp. 6–21; and G. P. Gooch, *History and Historians in the Nineteenth Century* (London, 1913), p. 343; Dockhorn, *op. cit.*, pp. 125–131.

30. Quoted by Gooch, *op. cit.*, p. 343.

31. Quoted by Dickins, *op. cit.*, p. 21.

32. The collected Papers of Frederic William Maitland, ed. H. A. L. Fisher, (Cambridge, 1911) III, p. 455. The whole passage is significant: "Would Englishmen see and understand what was happening in Germany? Would they appreciate and emulate the work of Savigny and Grimm?" And after the sentence given in the text: "We had our *guerrilleros*; they were valiant and resourceful; but in Germany an army was being organised."

33. William Holden Hutton, ed., *Letters of William Stubbs* (London, 1904) pp. 10, 16.

34. William Stubbs, *Two Lectures on the Present State and Prospects of Historical Study* (Oxford, 1876), pp. 7–8; and Hutton, pp. 264, 270.

35. Mrs. Louise Creighton, *Life and Letters of Mandell Creighton* (London, 1905), I, p. 51. Cf., Raymond Huntington Coon, *William*

Warde Fowler (Oxford, 1934), p. 27: "But lecturer and student alike, he says, were ignorant of history."

36. Stubbs, *op. cit.*, p. 42.

37. F. M. Powicke, ed., *Collected Papers of Thomas Frederick Tout* (Manchester, 1932), I, p. 76. J. H. Round wrote in agreement, p. 79.

38. See Sir Charles Oman, *Memories of Victorian Oxford* (Oxford, 1941), Ch. IX. Oman, like Tout and Round, studied with Stubbs; others included W. J. Ashley, C. H. Firth, and R. L. Poole. Creighton, among the tutors, was strongly influenced by him.

39. W. Stubbs, Seventeen Lectures on the Study of Medieval and Modern History 3rd ed. (Oxford, 1900) pp. 45–46.

40. In a generally sympathetic account given by Paul Fredericq in "The Study of History in England and Scotland," tr. Henrietta Leonard, *Johns Hopkins Studies in Historical and Political Science*, ed. Herbert Adams, 5th Series, No. x (Baltimore, 1887), p. 43, there is a comment on Stubbs' excuse for not organizing seminar study: 'he had not been an organizer because he hated organization and loved liberty,' which throws much light on the contrast between English and continental systems of education. "This argument against the practical course has several times confronted me in England. It surprised me in a country where colleges are emphatically organized communities and where lecturers are masters with whom the students are not considered able to dispense."

41. Stubbs, *op. cit.*, pp. 38–39. See also Dockhorn *op. cit.*, on Stubbs and the whole Oxford school, pp. 141 ff.

42. Stubbs, *op. cit.*, p. 40.

43. See Edward A. Freeman's *Lectures to American Audiences* (Philadelphia, 1864).

44. See "Memoir" by G. W. Prothero in J. R. Seeley, *The Growth of British Policy* (Cambridge, 1895). Cf., C. A. Bodelson, *Studies in Mid-Victorian Imperialism* (Kristiania, 1924), pp. 149–176.

45. Fredericq, *op. cit.*, pp. 16 ff.

46. Creighton, *op. cit.*, I, pp. 277–279; and Dockhorn, *op. cit.*, pp. 166–168. Among the tutors at Cambridge, G. W. Prothero (University of Bonn) was an admirer of Ranke and translated his *Weltgeschichte*.

47. Creighton, *op. cit.*, I, p. 333; H. A. L. Fisher, *James Bryce* (London, 1927), p. 194.

48. Creighton, *op. cit.*, I, pp. 264, 324; F. M. Müller, *Chips from a German Workshop*, III (London, 1890), p. 83.

49. Creighton, *op. cit.*, I, p. 334, and "Poole, Reginald Lane," *D. N. B.*

50. "Acton, Sir John Emerich Edward Dahlberg, 1st Baron Acton," *D. N. B.*

51. George Grote, *History of Greece* (London, 1862), "Preface of 1846," p. iv.

52. See the testimony of W. L. Newman before the Select Committee on the Oxford and Cambridge Education Bill, *PP*. 1867, XIII (C. 497), esp. his reply to Q. 1471. The study of Roman history was totally revised as a result of Theodor Mommsen's work, especially his *History of Rome* and the *Corpus of Latin Inscriptions*, by J. L. Strachan-Davidson, H. F. Pelham, and William Warde Fowler, among others. See Henry Francis Pelham, *Essays*, ed. F. Haverfield (Oxford, 1911), esp. p. xvi.

53. Müller, *op. cit.*, II, *passim*.

54. *Ibid.*, II, p. 275.

55. Beatrice Webb, *op. cit.* (note 15, Chapter I above), pp. 80, 86.

56. Müller, *op. cit.*, I, pp. 336–337.

57. *Ibid.*, I, p. 414.

58. See for example a late instance: Goldwin Smith, "The Greatness of England," *Contemporary Review*, 34 (1878–79), pp. 1–18.

59. Benjamin Lippincott, *Victorian Critics of Democracy* (Minneapolis, Minn., 1938), p. 142, quoting from Leslie Stephen, *Life of James Fitzjames Stephen*.

60. Quoted by Lippincott, p. 143, from James Fitzjames Stephen, *Liberty, Equality, Fraternity* (London, 1874), p. 31.

61. Lippincott, *op. cit.*, pp. 142–143.

62. John Stuart Mill, *Autobiography* (London, 1924), pp. 177–179.

63. Paul Vinogradoff, *Collected Papers*, ed. H. A. L. Fisher (Oxford, 1928), II, p. 180. Cf., Frederick Pollock, *Oxford Lectures and Other Discourses* (London, 1890); W. S. Holdsworth, *The Historians of Anglo-American Law* (New York, 1928); Dockhorn, *op. cit.*, pp. 172 ff.

64. Henry Sumner Maine, *Ancient Law* (London, 1861), p. 118.

65. *Ibid.*, p. 116: "Even if they [primitive societies] gave more trouble than they do, no pains would be wasted in ascertaining the germs out of which has assuredly been unfolded every form of moral restraint which controls and shapes our conduct at the present moment." Note the typical assumption of the German theory of a development by unfolding from a 'germ.'

66. Quoted by Lippincott, *op. cit.*, p. 176.

67. James Bryce, *Legal Studies in the University of Oxford* (London, 1893), p. 5.

68. "Maitland, Frederic William," *D. N. B.*

69. R. R. Marett, *Taylor* (New York, 1936), pp. 69–70.

70. *Ibid.*, p. 28 and note, pp. 62, 89, 198.

71. *Ibid.*, pp. 44–50.

72. *Ibid.*, p. 25.

73. "James Mark" D.N.B. (1922–30), pp. 884–7.

74. See R. Angus Downie, *James George Frazer* (London, 1940), esp. pp. 10–11. Cf., R. R. Marett, "James George Frazer, 1854–1941," *Proceedings of the British Academy*, XXVII (1941).

75. Marett, *Tylor*, p. 16.

76. J. S. Keltie, "Geographical Education," *Supplementary Papers*, I, Part IV, Royal Geographical Society (London, 1886), 439–594.

77. *Ibid.*, p. 474.

78. *Ibid.*, p. 475.

79. G. Tatham, "Geography in the Nineteenth Century," in *Geography in the Twentieth Century*, ed. T. Griffith Taylor (New York, 1953), pp. 28–69.

80. H. J. Mackinder, "Modern Geography, German and English," *The Geographical Journal*, 6 (1895), p. 371.

81. *Ibid.*, p. 367.

82. *Ibid.*, p. 376.

The Professionalization of the Sciences

The belief that British fear of German industrial competition was first seriously aroused only in the eighties,[1] though true for the majority of business men, politicians, and journalists, ignores an important segment of English opinion. That German competition in trade would sooner or later become a threat to Britain's industrial supremacy had long been foreseen by British scientists and scholars who had either been trained in German laboratories and seminars, come under the influence of Prince Albert, or had discovered for themselves Germany's remarkable educational development.[2] These scientists and scholars, supported by a few industrialists, began in 1867 to awaken and stimulate British fear of the German trade rivalry. Aided by the military victories of Prussia in 1866 and 1870, and the trade depression of the mid-seventies, they raised the alarm in order to persuade their fellow-countrymen of the necessity of supporting education generally and instruction in the sciences particularly. They knew that England had fallen behind in both. The educational awakening England experienced in the two decades between the passage of the Second Reform Bill and the Jubilee year must be largely attributed to these men, and through them to the German influence.

Three phases of activity on behalf of scientific instruction can be distinguished in these two decades: a reform of the old and the founding of new institutions of learning at the college level, the introduction of laboratory instruction in the sciences, and the extension of technical education. Of these, the second was of greatest importance, since without it the others would have been next to worthless, and since this was the one most directly influenced by the Germans. But they were interrelated in that all of them reflected and encouraged the growth of specialized research, and technological expertness with their inevitable accompaniment of professionalism, and the German influence was an active stimulus in all.

1.

German competition renews interest in education and science

Until the Austro-Prussian War, little attention was paid the Germanies by Englishmen generally. But immediately thereafter, the International Exhibition in Paris led them to an uneasy recognition of Germany's prowess in industry as well as in war. Among those exercised by the superiority of both the German and the French to the English exhibits was Lyon Playfair. In the course of a discussion with the English jurors at the Exhibition, he was persuaded to address a letter on the subject to the Taunton School Inquiry Commission. It was accompanied by a letter from Lord Granville in which the latter associated the "lessons which the late war in Germany and the present Exhibition in Paris afforded us."[3] The Commission circulated Playfair's letter among the English jurors for comment. Of the sixteen men to whom the letter went, fourteen agreed, with minor reservations, that the neglect of education in science and technology ("science and industrial arts") by England was "permitting other nations to advance in industry at a much greater rate than our own country," and supported Playfair's suggestion for a government commission to make an official inquiry on the subject.[4]

Two industrialists, Anthony J. Mundella and Bernhard Samuelson, appeared as allies for the scientists. Mundella was a partner in a large hosiery concern at Nottingham. On visiting the city of Chemnitz in Saxony, where his firm had a branch, "what he saw there led him to study closely the educational system of Saxony, Prussia, and other states."[5] Mundella was one of those to whom Playfair's letter was sent by the Taunton Commission. In reply he wrote, "The contrast betwixt the workpeople of England and Saxony, engaged in the same industry, is humiliating."[6] Elected to Parliament by the newly enfranchised workers of Sheffield, he became a devoted supporter of public education. Samuelson, German-born but taken to England as a child, was an iron manufacturer with considerable experience in continental business. Alarmed by the advances made in Germany, in 1867 he undertook a private investigation of technical instruction in Belgium, France, Switzerland, and Germany.[7]

On a motion by Samuelson, a Select Committee was appointed by the Commons in 1868 to investigate technical education abroad.[8] Its report included Samuelson's account of his own survey, in which he wrote almost lyrically of the German technical higher schools; a long study by Professor Leone Levi of King's College, London, in which a great expansion of scientific and technical training facilities was recommended; and reports from Britain's official representatives abroad, which were circulated for the committee by Lord Stanley of the Foreign Office.[9] This represented the first serious effort made by Parliament to study the comparative position of English technical education and led to public discussions in the principal cities of Britain.[10]

Other testimony supported this report. In 1868 Matthew Arnold's study of continental schools and universities was published with its sharp warning of Germany's industrial and commercial success in the new era, the characteristics of which he clearly foresaw.[11] J. Scott Russell, naval architect and "disciple of the Prince Consort," published in 1869 a book on technical education and England's danger from the better trained Continentals.[12]

When on 17 February 1870 W. E. Forster of Gladstone's Cabinet presented to the Commons his Elementary Education Bill, this was very largely to meet the demands for technical education for the workers. Ever since 1853, when a commission had visited the New York Industrial Exhibition, the demand for a national system of compulsory education had been continuous.[13] But it was this latest agitation which turned the scales. In introducing the bill, Forster argued that elementary education was a necessary preliminary to technical education. Referring to the examples of the United States and Germany and to the work of the member for

Birmingham (Mr. Dixon) and the member for Sheffield (Mr. Mundella) in stimulating zeal for education, he urged: "We must not delay. Upon the speedy provision of elementary education depends our industrial prosperity. It is of no use trying to give technical teaching to our artizans without elementary education; uneducated labourers—and many of our labourers are utterly uneducated—are, for the most part, unskilled labourers, and if we leave our work-folk any longer unskilled . . . they will become over-matched in the competition of the world."[14] Already, it is clear that one of the forces to which Forster felt he could appeal directly was the fear of German competition associated with technical education.

In the debate, Dixon argued for the program of the Birmingham Education League: compulsory, free education and a department of education headed by a minister. To Lord Robert Montagu, who insisted that education was already amply provided for, Mundella replied: "He should like to ask hon. Members what they meant when they talked about education. In Germany the term signified that the child had been at school from six to fourteen years of age; but some persons in this country seemed to imagine that it was sufficient for the child's name to have once appeared on the school books for its education to be completed."[15]

The Education Act of 1870 arranged for the public provision of elementary education, where it was not already available, for the laboring population. It was not designed to replace existing facilities, nor to provide for the middle or upper classes. It did not make elementary education either compulsory or free; education became compulsory to the age of twelve and half-time to the age of fourteen only with Mundella's Act of 1880. But with the old apprenticeship methods becoming outmoded, technical training was increasingly required and elementary education was therefore necessary. As the technical exploits of the United States had stimulated the demand for a public educational system, the German model and the rising fear of German competition reconciled the English to such state intervention as seemed inevitable.

Meanwhile in 1869 Norman Lockyer had founded the general scientific journal *Nature* and entered upon his long and arduous campaign for the promotion of scientific research and education.[16]

Nature's importance was that it provided a medium through which opinion among British scientists could be formulated and communicated. For though there were in existence journals publishing scientific papers, they did little to create a sense of professional fellowship and responsibility such as a weekly could promote.

To do this had been since its founding one of the aims of the British Association for the Advancement of Science,[17] but in England in the nineteenth century professionalism was suspect. An important article of the laissez-faire creed held that professionalism was monopolistic and encouraged "exclusiveness, selfishness, and sloth."[18] The guilds had long since dwindled into social relics, and study associations were extremely heterogeneous in membership, often including as many non-scientific as scientific men.[19] England remained the country of the amateur, and specialization continued to be regarded as not quite gentlemanly.

From the first issue, *Nature* reflected in its columns the admiration of informed British scientists for the excellence of Germany's educational system from the lowest grades through the universities, for her scientific laboratories, and her scientific achievements. Contrasts drawn between German scientific institutions and achievements and those of the British consistently pointed to the superiority of the former. The need for reform and diffusion of education in England became a major concern.

Interest in the subject having been awakened, in May of 1870, a Royal Commission on Scientific Instruction and the Advancement of Science was appointed.[20] It was known as the Devonshire Commission for William Cavendish, Seventh Duke of Devonshire, who served as chairman. Norman Lockyer was appointed its secretary, and through the pages of *Nature*, he kept its work before the scientific public. The other members were Lord Lansdowne, Sir John Lubbock, James Kay-Shuttleworth, Bernhard Samuelson, William Sharpey, Thomas Henry Huxley, George Gabriel Stokes, and William A. Miller, replaced on his death by Henry J. S. Smith.[21] For five years this Commission sat, taking evidence from a diversity of industrial, educational, and scientific authorities. Its eight reports furnished voluminous evidence of extraordinary variety, and with that variety, the woeful inadequacy of scientific instruction available in the United Kingdom.[22] The incompleteness, due to the lack of any systematic program of instruction even in the two oldest universities, the wealth and power of the Colleges at Oxford and Cambridge and the poverty and impotence of the university professors and officers; the financial stringency of the London Colleges, University and King's, and of Owens College, Manchester; the elementary level of scientific instruction available even in the more advanced schools; and the difficulty the best trained men had in finding time and facilities for research were spread on the record for all to see.

That the Commissioners feared that the scientific advances on the Continent would soon affect Britain's industrial leadership is evident from the direction taken by their questions to the industrialists and engineers.[23] The leadership in German science and technology and, after her, France was repeatedly pointed out by the scientists appearing before them. Many of the most eminent scientists in the kingdom were questioned and, with the single exception of George Biddell Airy, the aging Astronomer Royal, who found all existing arrangements satisfactory, affirmed their support of greatly increased government aid to science and scientific instruction.[24]

But the Commission's recommendations went much further. "These considerations . . . have impressed upon us," the Commissioners wrote, "the conviction that the Creation of a Special Ministry dealing with Science and with Education is a Necessity of the Public Service."[25] The Minister should be assisted by a board. As Lockyer reported in *Nature*, a division of opinion existed among the scientists concerning the organization of this board. "Two modes may be suggested in which such a board might be organised. First, the Government might formally recognise the President and Council of the Royal Society as its official adviser, imposing the whole responsibility on that body, and leaving it to them to seek advice when necessary . . . The second method would be to create an entirely new board, somewhat after the model of the old Board of Longitude, but with improvements."[26] The Commissioners thought "the balance of argument and authority" favored the latter and it was this, accordingly, that they recommended.[27]

If, as Lord Salisbury remarked to the Commissioners, state aid to science could be justified out of Adam Smith, it was a Conservative who made the remark, and these proposals looked far beyond state aid. This recommendation called for a greater expansion of government activity than had the Birmingham proposals for elementary education to be provided for by the state. It implied government supervision of science research, and instruction in all its branches.[28] Nor could even the Conservative politicians, Lord Salisbury and Lord Derby, bring themselves to the point of advocating a minister and council for the sciences through the modest Parliamentary grant administered by the Royal Society.[29]

To the scientists, at least, what had often been said and yet only partially understood in its full potentiality, i.e. that science was power, was becoming only too evident. In an editorial in 1870, entitled "Scientific Administration," Lockyer declared that the Prussians "are emphatically a scientific people," and credited their new military triumphs "to that predominating characteristic." The word "science" implies, he wrote, "simply the employment of means adequate to the attainment of a desired end. Whether that end be the constitution of a government, the organisation of an army or navy, the spread of learning, or the repression of crime." He insisted that: "The same method is necessary to raise, organise, and equip a battalion, as to perform a chemical experiment. It is this great truth that the Germans, above all other nations, if not alonest among nations, have thoroughly realised and applied." This was conspicuously lacking among the English. "As a nation, we have never realised the necessity for system and completeness in utilising our material resources."[30]

About this description of the cultural characteristics of the two peoples there is nothing new; we have long been accustomed to regarding the Germans as systematic, methodical, thorough, and the English as a people who "muddle through." But in 1870 this was startling in its reversal of the general opinion,[31] yet it was also almost undeniable, at least as concerned the Germans, in the face of the sudden revelation of their armed might. No longer could the Germans be dismissed as a nation content with metaphysics, music, beer, and the petty politics of provincial courts. Almost overnight Germany had risen to the position of a first-rate power, deceptively liberal in government, a leader in scholarship and science, and a challenger by virtue of her industrial potential. It was their recognition of the extraordinary increase in power won by the Germans through organization and systematic study that led Lyon Playfair, T. H. Huxley, Matthew Arnold, J. Norman Lockyer, Henry Enfield Roscoe, E. Ray Lankester and, in addition to the industrialists Mundella and Samuelson, Philip Magnus to stress the German example, and to seek to arouse the English from their long lethargy regarding education, especially in regard to the sciences and technologies. A beginning was made between 1867 and 1871. The report of the Select Committee, the debates on the Education Bill, and the reports of the Devonshire Commission undoubtedly led many Englishmen to look to German competition as an explanation, however partial, for the depression of 1874–79, when fear of German commercial rivalry first appeared in business and journalistic circles. This fear was to be brushed aside when recovery from the depression appeared imminent in the latter year.

2.

Founding of the city colleges

Attacks upon Oxford and Cambridge in the 1870's were frequent and harsh and, from the viewpoint of the scientists, warranted by their failure to keep abreast intellectually with the German universities. At this time they were still the principal institutions of higher learning in England. The degree-granting University of London served as an examining body, after 1858, for any individual no matter where he had prepared but specifically for those prepared by numerous small collegiate institutions. Of these, only University College and King's College, London, and Owens College, Manchester, were of any considerable importance. But the ferment produced by the fear of German competition and the work of the scientific commissions in exposing the weakness of Oxford and Cambridge, combined with an increased interest in education, resulting from the extension of suffrage, led to the founding of many new colleges which were eventually to achieve university status—the now familiar "Redbrick" or civic universities.

Until 1867, and in many ways for years thereafter, provisions for instruction in the sciences were paltry in both the ancient universities when compared with those in most German universities. Particularly obnoxious in the eyes of the reformers was the control of great wealth by the colleges and the poverty of the universities. Funds of close to £100,000 went yearly in the form of fellowships to young men who succeeded in passing with distinction such examinations as their college tutors set them. These fellowships were tenable for life, whether the holders engaged in work at the universities or preferred to regard the money as a simple annuity, continued celibacy being the principal requirement. Meanwhile the university authorities lacked money to supply either laboratories or lecturers in the sciences.[32] The professorships were also held for life and more than one appointment might be held by one man even though he did not necessarily reside at the university or teach.[33] Such a situation invited attack, particularly by those who were familiar with the German universities. The result was to exert strong pressure to reform the old universities and to promote the founding of the new colleges.

It has frequently been said that the two ancient universities were "reformed from within" during this period but the statement is at best partial and misleading. Though it is true that many of the professors and tutors of both universities were active in behalf of some change, it may be doubted that they would have had much success had their efforts not been assisted by outsiders and especially by the Devonshire Commission and the Commissions for the Universities of the late seventies.[34] This was particularly true in the case of Oxford. Insofar as reform came from within, however, those most active in the cause of reform were usually men who admired, or had studied in, the German universities. Opponents of reform continually taunted the reformers with wishing to make the universities into Prussianized institutions.[35]

An example of the efforts of the reformers was a meeting held in London on 16 November 1872, "by members of the Universities and others interested in the promotion of mature study and scientific research in England."[36] Presiding was Mark Pattison, Rector of Lincoln College, Oxford, a staunch reformer, strongly influenced by the German system.[37] Among those participating were George Rolleston and Benjamin Brodie, also of Oxford, historian J. R. Seeley of Cambridge, T. H. Huxley and W. T. Thiselton-Dyer of the Royal School of Mines, W. K. Clifford, W. B. Carpenter, and John Burdon-Sanderson of University College, London. Discussion centered on the system of fellowships, the desirability of a graded teaching body composed of scholars with a specialist's knowledge of the subject, and the need of facilities for research, especially in the sciences.[38]

Shortly thereafter, Brodie contributed to *Nature* an article, "Scientific Research and University Endowments," which probably reflected his remarks at the November meeting.[39] After condemning the sinecure fellowships, he found that science was handicapped in England "by the utter apathy in regard to the advancement of knowledge which has so long prevailed at the English Universities, which, without any doubt, is the main cause of our disasters." The English situation was in sorry contrast to conditions in Germany where "the universities are the very centers of intellectual progress." Throughout these decades such attacks appeared in *Nature* time and again.

The characteristic theme during the depression of the mid-seventies was sounded by Thomas Andrews in his presidential address before the British Association for the Advancement of Science meeting in Glasgow in 1876. "It may perhaps appear to many," he said, "a paradoxical assertion to maintain that the industries of the country should look to the calm and serene regions of Oxford and Cambridge for help in the troublous times of which we have now a sharp and severe note of warning. But I have not spoken on light grounds . . . If Great Britain is to retain the commanding position she has so long occupied in skilled manufacture, the easy ways . . . which have sufficed for the past will not be found to suffice for the future. The highest training which can be brought to bear on practical science will be imperatively required; and it will be a fatal policy if that training is to be sought for in foreign lands because it cannot be obtained at home." And after citing at length the example of the University of Berlin and German education generally, he concluded: "The outlay which is incurred by any country for the promotion of science and of high instruction will yield a certain return; and Germany has not had long to wait for the ingathering of the fruits of her far-sighted policy."[40]

The most devastating attack came, however, from E. Ray Lankester, a Fellow of Exeter College, Oxford, and professor of zoology at University College, London. Published in full in the *British Medical Journal*,[41] his address was summarized in *Nature*.[42] After deploring the status of medical study in Britain, Lankester described in detail the situation at the small University of Heidelberg, which was supported by the Grand Duchy of Baden. Referring briefly to the other German universities, he noted that Berlin "possesses laboratories and museums on a palatial scale, and a perfect army of investigators and students supported by State endowment." Contrasting England's small provision for scientific research, he turned to criticism of Oxford and Cambridge. Particularly bitter were several passages dealing with the diversion of endowments by the colleges from the scientific purposes intended by the donors, and he cited names and instances.

Meanwhile the Devonshire Commission was issuing its reports. The Third Report, largely devoted to Oxford and Cambridge, drew a direct contrast between the schedules of courses at the two English universities and colleges with that of the University of Berlin.[43] Though noting the recent advances made, the Commissioners concluded that teaching in the sciences was inadequate, requiring a greater "plurality of teachers" in order to achieve a necessary "breadth and depth of instruction." They further recommended, and called attention to this recommendation again in their Seventh Report of two years later, stating that the degree of Doctor in Science be instituted for which original research should be made a requirement (as in German universities), a requirement also recommended to be made conditional to the awarding of fellowships.[44]

The reports of the Devonshire and other parliamentary commissions of the 1870's and the various attacks aided, as we shall see, in bringing about some reform in the ancient universities. But they also probably contributed to the founding of the new institutions of higher learning. For it is more than likely that few of the middle-class industrialists had any conception earlier of the true situation existing in the sciences and technologies in the old universities. Partly, since many were Dissenters, they distrusted the universities as the home of Anglicanism; yet it was not until the religious tests were abolished at Oxford and Cambridge that they founded the city colleges. More significant is the fact that without exception the new institutions stressed the sciences and all included laboratory work from the outset. In any event it was not until the attacks on the two universities became general and fear of German competition was aroused that English industrialists founded and supported institutions of higher learning in which a curriculum better adapted to meet the needs of an industrial society and less expensively addicted to the delights of high living and light learning would predominate.[45]

The dates of the founding of the new colleges tell their own tale: Armstrong College, Newcastle-on-Tyne (a branch of Durham University, primarily an Anglican theological school), 1871; Yorkshire College of Science, Leeds, 1874; College of Science for the West of England, Bristol, 1876; Firth College, Sheffield, 1879; Mason's College of Science, Birmingham, 1880; Nottingham College of Science, 1881; and University College, Liverpool, 1882. With the exception of Nottingham, all of these colleges were affiliated with medical schools having facilities for clinical instruction.[46]

One of the first to respond to the new impulse was Henry Roscoe, the German-trained chemist of Owens College. Stimulated by the report of the Taunton Commission, Roscoe together with Principal Greenwood of Owens College, visited Germany and Switzerland in 1868 to study the universities and polytechnical higher schools.[47] Upon his return he wrote two articles for *Nature*. In the first he contrasted the so-called "free" English system of university education with the German. German universities were, in the main, open "without limitation of number [or] religious test of any kind, and for the payment of ridiculously low fees." He stressed also the excellence of the German physical, chemical, and physiological laboratories, and the connection of the medical schools both with hospitals, as in England, and with the universities.[48] In his second treatise, he dealt with "The Polytechnical Schools," questioning the separation of the technical from the purely scientific, and quoting Liebig in support of his doubts.[49] Probably it was due to his effort that the Manchester Council of Arts Society resolved "That the best interests of the country demanded the establishment of a complete system of primary education, the extension of the system science classes under a responsible department of the Government, and under a definite plan, and especially the establishment of science colleges in the principal industrial centers of the United Kingdom."[50] Roscoe also set to work to improve the facilities of Owens College so that it might assume full university rank, perhaps the easier in Manchester because the "German influence was very strong there."[51] Success came when in 1880 Owens College was chartered as Victoria University with the understanding that Leeds and Liverpool would shortly become other colleges of the new university.

The beginnings of another college are traced to the visit to the Paris Exhibition of Thomas Nussey of Leeds whose report urged the need of technical education in England.[52] Two years later G. H. Nussey and A. Nussey founded the Leeds Art and Science Institute from which developed the Yorkshire College of Science.[53] At Bristol, the circular calling a meeting in 1874 to discuss the founding of a university college read: "It is generally admitted that the prosperity of British industry must in future greatly depend upon the proper scientific and technical training of those by whom the commerce and manufactures of the country will be carried out."[54]

Following the example already set by Owens College and the two London colleges, the new institutions were organized more on the Scottish and German than on the English university model in having professorial teaching; being city colleges, they rarely had any boarding-houses. To claim direct German influence in each instance would be preposterous. But the widely and continuously cited German example, the intensively fostered fear of German industrial competition, and the German experience of many of the leading teachers played important roles in providing an impulse, otherwise so long delayed as to be almost inexplicable.[55] Many of the new colleges had their start as either centers of adult education or as mechanics' institutes, but so marked was the preoccupation with the sciences and technical training that even the leading exponents of scientific instruction felt called upon occasionally to protest.

For despite the bitterness of their attacks upon the ancient universities, it is worth recalling that none of the leaders in this movement were irresponsible fanatics or radical politicians. They were not carried away by Saint-Simonian or Comtean dreams of a state directed by scientists or an intellectual elite, and if they had little patience with what they dubbed metaphysics or mysticism, none among them deprecated the humanities or liberal arts in the curriculum of either colleges or universities. More than once Lockyer reiterated what he wrote upon the inauguration of the Yorkshire College of Science. "We do not want a Yorkshire College of Science, but a Yorkshire College in which science will be found in its proper place. It must be remembered that the whole duty of these local colleges is not limited to the instruction in the particular sciences which more directly relate to the manufacturing industries of the districts in which they are placed; they must be made to act as *nuclei* for higher culture by the establishment of chairs of Art and Literature."[56] The scientists also continually urged the importance of providing facilities for research as well as for instruction. If this was true of the scientists who were not Oxford or Cambridge men, it must be unnecessary to add that this was the position of men such as Arnold, Pattison, Jowett, Brodie, and many others. What they were all combating was the ignorance of the many and blind subservience to the past, while simultaneously attempting to raise the standards and extend the curriculum of education generally. By failing to maintain a position of intellectual leadership in the advancement of the sciences, Cambridge and Oxford had neglected their national responsibilities. The German competition and the German example compelled reform and the founding of supplementary institutions. For it was the genuine achievements of the Germans that rendered them an object of envy, as it was the complacency of the English that rendered German competition a danger.

3.

German influence in physiology, botany, and zoology

In J. Reynolds Green's *A History of Botany in the United Kingdom*, the heading for the chapter dealing with the two decades 1870–1890 is "The Coming of the Laboratory."[57] The introduction of the laboratory, and the original investigation which accompanied it in the more advanced institutions, marked a turning point in scientific instruction in England. For the coming of the laboratory was not restricted to botanical study. Though the principal sciences had been represented by professorships in the English universities, the teaching, when any was performed, was either wholly theoretical, with occasional demonstrations, or, if devoted at all to "practical work" (not required for a degree), took place in one of the very few existing teaching laboratories, which were cramped and poorly equipped. Despite the recommendations of the Royal Commissions for the Universities of the fifties, little had been accomplished before 1867.

It was immediately after that year that changes began to be initiated. The first encouragement to scientific study came with the building of the Clarendon Laboratory and the Cavendish Laboratory at Cambridge. A few of the colleges at Oxford and Cambridge founded small laboratories as well. After Michael Foster had been teaching several years, a physiological laboratory was instituted for him in the late seventies, and one was built for J. Burdon-Sanderson upon his appointment to Oxford in 1882. After delays and difficulties, botanical laboratories also appeared, and in 1885, at Cambridge, a laboratory for organic chemistry was founded. To staff it, a German organic chemist, Siegfried Ruhemann, was brought in on the recommendation of August von Hofmann of Berlin.[58] At the London colleges the laboratories were enlarged, and the University of London founded a laboratory of pathology in which Burdon-Sanderson, Edward Klein, and Victor Horsley, among others, worked.[59] New science buildings with laboratories were erected in the early seventies by Owens College,[60] and the new colleges, consciously scientific in orientation, provided laboratories of sorts from their founding.

Even the erection of laboratories could not, however, solve England's problems in scientific instruction at once. Both adequately prepared teachers and students were lacking. The difficulties confronting the older universities as well as the new colleges in introducing anything beyond elementary work may be illustrated by the experience of James Clerk Maxwell as professor of experimental physics in the new Cavendish Laboratory. During the six years of his teaching (1874–79), only a few students worked in the laboratory.[61] Attendance at his lectures was greater, particularly in the early years, but in 1878, we are told, two or three students attended and the following year only two, an Englishman and an American. The reason was obvious. Few English students were prepared to understand advanced work and Maxwell "had too much learning and too much originality to be at his best in elementary teaching."[62]

Neither was a laboratory of much use to the trained scientist in charge if he had to devote all his time to elementary teaching.[63] As a writer in *Nature* observed: "Now . . . we have a goodly number of chemical schools rising up, with in many cases professors trained in German laboratories. But in many of these the professor . . . has too much routine teaching and too little time for original work."[64]

In the biological sciences, the situation was very different from that in chemistry: physiology, zoology, and botany were hardly modern sciences as practiced in England before 1867.[65] What was particularly required was a new group of men with a vision of these as experimental sciences. The Germans furnished the vision and a notable group of men appeared, aware of the German experimental methods and the German achievements, or themselves trained in German laboratories.

Thomas Huxley was a remarkable figure in the English scientific scene of the mid-years of the century. Apart from his support of Darwin and his campaign in behalf of technical education, he stood nearly alone in the character of his scientific interest. "There was very little of the genuine naturalist in me," he wrote. "I never collected anything and species work was a burden to me. What I cared for was the architectural and engineering part of the business."[66] How revealing this is of the generally prevailing conception of the natural scientist in mid-Victorian England: the naturalist was a collector and systematist, and that was the sum total of his "science." Huxley's very different interest made him seek to understand the functional as well as the formal relationships and, stimulated by his reading in Johannes Müller and Karl von Baer,[67] he was led inevitably into the experimental laboratory and to dissatisfaction with a teaching method which in addition to the lectures consisted, at most, of demonstrations. The result was his founding of the "great course" in biology at South Kensington in 1871, the course which, in Green's words, "Coming as it did side by side with the dawning influence of the German school . . . prepared the way for a total revolution in the methods of botanical study,"[68] and for something similar in the study of physiology and zoology.

Until 1870 there were few teaching laboratories in physiology. Largely responsible for the existing ones was William Sharpey of University College, London.[69] Determined to introduce laboratory teaching, he persuaded George Harley, who had worked in Paris with Claude Bernard, to start such a class. But Harley's practice as a physician led him to give up the enterprise and Sharpey turned to one of his students, Michael Foster, whom he induced to give up the practice of medicine for the purpose. Foster's appointment to University College, London, according to Sir Edward Sharpey-Schafer "proved a decisive factor in the history of physiology in England."[70] Together with Sharpey, Foster toured the continental laboratories to study the work being done in France and Germany. The success of his laboratory class encouraged a few others to similar undertakings. Among them was F. William Pavy, another student of Bernard's, at Guy's Hospital; and Foster's successor at University College, John Burdon-Sanderson. The latter was also a physician who had studied chemistry with Gerhardt and Würtz, embryology with Coste, and physiology with Bernard.[71] The importance of the work of the physiologists in Germany appeared, however, not only in its own subject matter or in relation to medicine, but also in relation to botany, zoology, and psychology, and it was perhaps with the last especially in mind that George Henry Lewes, (himself familiar with the German work), and George Eliot suggested to their friend, philologist W. G. Clark, the need for establishing the study of experimental physiology at Cambridge. Clark, George M. Humphrey, George Paget, and Coutts Trotter, the last of whom had studied with von Helmholtz, persuaded Trinity College to found a praelectorship in physiology. At Huxley's suggestion, Michael Foster was appointed to the post.[72] Few appointments have more profoundly influenced the future of a university or a subject.

But Foster's work was also to profit from Huxley's "great course." Designed to provide science teachers for the elementary schools resulting from the Education Act of 1870, the course was given for the first time in the summer of 1871 on the ground floor of the yet-unfinished South Kensington Museum. Huxley's course consisted of a series of hour-long lectures in the morning and four hours of laboratory work in the afternoon, for which he imported a number of assistants.[73] The significance of the course was not that it was one of the first in which laboratory teaching was employed in the natural sciences in England.[74] The "great course" was distinctive for its inclusion of both plants and animals, its emphasis on a systematic use of types of organisms, and its greater attention to microscopic forms. Of still more importance, however, was the guidance and opportunity the course offered to the remarkable group of men brought in as laboratory instructors. Among the first were Michael Foster, William Rutherford, and E. Ray Lankester; later, when it had become an established course, with the transfer of the School of Mines to South Kensington, came William Thiselton-Dyer, Newell Martin, Sydney Vines, and others.[75]

The direct result of the course and of the German influence was the founding of two important centers of botanical study in England, one at Cambridge and one at Kew Gardens. To these was added the Oxford School, though it never attained the importance of the other two. Another result was that the course promoted and contributed to the success of the Cambridge school of physiology and zoology. More generally, it may be said to have revolutionized the teaching of the natural sciences in England by inaugurating the training of a professoriate in the biological sciences for the United Kingdom and the Dominions.

After Claude Bernard's laboratory, itself of first importance, the great center of physiological study in Europe was the laboratory of Karl Ludwig. Many of England's leading physiologists had studied with him.[76] And it was frequently from the Cambridge school of physiology founded by Michael Foster[77] that these students went on to the Continent.[78] Of the older men, J. Burdon-Sanderson's background has already been noted. E. Ray Lankester had also had extensive foreign training, having studied with Rokitansky in Vienna and A. F. Dohrn at the Naples Biological Station, as well as with Ludwig. His teaching career, after a short period at Oxford, continued at University College, London, followed by a return to Oxford, and finally at the British Institution, London.[79]

Because of Huxley's illness, in 1873 W. Thiselton-Dyer, assisted by Lawson, professor of botany at Oxford, headed the course at South Kensington and gave additional attention to the botanical side. To indicate the source of his inspiration his own words are best:

> At the time I shared the general belief that the manipulative difficulties were so great in demonstrating the things to be seen in [German] textbooks that only men like Hofmeister could accomplish it. I was shaken in this belief at the British Association in Edinburgh in 1871, when Prof. A. Dickson had a remarkable exhibit . . . He was, I think, the first of our botanists to get an inspiration in original work from Germany . . . I was very keen to demonstrate what Hofmeister had done . . . It would have seemed hopeless if Casimir de Candolle had not come to England after working with Strasburger, and brought a number of preparations with him. He showed me that the difficulties were not insuperable.[80]

The leading figures in botany in Germany were Wilhelm Hofmeister, A. H. de Bary at Strasbourg, and J. von Sachs at Würzburg. The principal founders of scientific botany in England studied either at Strasbourg or Würzburg and often at both.[81]

In 1875 Thiselton-Dyer became Assistant Director of Kew Gardens under his father-in-law, Joseph Dalton Hooker. There he was instrumental in inaugurating the study of physiological botany which led ultimately to the founding of the Jodrell Laboratory at Kew. Many English botanists worked with him at one time or another, including William McNab, afterwards professor at Dublin, and Hick, who went to Manchester.[82]

Associated with Thiselton-Dyer at Kensington in 1874 was Sydney Vines who had studied at Cambridge with Foster. After Vines began teaching at Cambridge himself, he studied both at Strasbourg and Würzburg. His success at Cambridge equalled that of Foster, who aided him as much as possible, even providing him with laboratory room he could himself ill afford to spare. As Demonstrator, responsible for both lectures and laboratory work as late as 1880, Vines was finally promoted to Reader. But when in 1887 Bailey Balfour went to Edinburgh, and Vines was offered the professorship of botany at Oxford, he accepted, since the erstwhile professor of botany at Cambridge, Charles Babbington, though no longer either residing or teaching, was still living. In the meantime, Vines had created a flourishing department assisted, after 1882, by Francis Darwin.[83]

It was not, however, only directly through study in Germany that the German influence operated; the texts in the natural sciences were for many years almost exclusively in German or were translations from that language.[84] One of Thiselton-Dyer's important contributions was to edit Alfred W. Bennett's translation of Sach's *Lehrbuch* in 1875;[85] and A. W. Ward published a translation of Sach's *Lectures on Physiology* in 1887.[86] In 1885 Vines and Bower published a *Handbook of Practical Botany* and the following year Vines' *Physiology of Plants* appeared, "the first contribution of an Englishman to the new botanical literature."[87] To mark their new departures, the new schools also founded their own journals. In 1878 Foster started the *Journal of Physiology;*[88] and in 1887 Balfour and Vines initiated the *Annals of Botany*.[89] Partly to counter the anti-vivisectionist agitation, the leaders in physiology founded the Physiological Society in 1876.[90]

One of the triumphs of the biologists was almost wholly the result of E. Ray Lankester's efforts. As we have seen, he and a number of other English zoologists had studied with the German Dohrn at the Naples Marine Biological Station. Following a fisheries exhibition, Lankester began agitating for an English marine biological station, such as the leading Continental states already had. Lockyer promptly supported the proposal in *Nature*, and at the suggestion of Dr. Günther of the British Museum, the Marine Biological Association was founded with Huxley as president and Lankester as secretary. The Association raised a considerable sum of money by subscription with the participation of the City Companies. In addition, the government was persuaded to contribute £5,000 and to supply an annual subsidy of £500. The result was the founding of the Plymouth Biological Station in 1887 with G. C. Bourne, who had studied in the laboratory of August Weismann, Freiburg im Breisgau, as first director.[91]

From 1867 to 1887, as a result of strong German influence, England began to lay the foundations for education in science and technology. English scientists ceased to be largely amateurs, and the leaders in the professionalization of the sciences were usually either German-trained or conscious of following German leadership. Before the founding of the new colleges and laboratories, opportunities of employment for experimental scientists were, even in teaching, so few as to discourage all but the ablest and most determined. But despite this gradual development of a professorship in the sciences, a lack of technologists, as well as a widespread indifference to the advantage of employing them, was still to characterize English industry for many years to come.

4.

German influence in technical education

When a new depression in trade began in 1884, the business community and the politicians became for the first time seriously alarmed by the competition of Germany. Nearly two decades of ceaseless preaching on the theme of German science and education and its effect upon industry was finally making a serious impression. Businessmen began to demand consular assistance to traders abroad; they developed a greater interest in trade with the colonies. In the face of the new tariffs of Germany and France, a Fair Trade movement, urging tariff retaliation, gained momentum in England. In 1887 Parliament was persuaded to pass the Merchandise Marks Act, which put the famous mark "Made in Germany" on all goods manufactured there. It was expected to reveal the inferiority of German-made goods. The English were instead shocked to discover how widely and successfully German-made goods were competing even in the home market.[92]

Willing as the businessmen were to call upon the government for assistance in some ways, many of them doubtless agreed with the remarks made by a physician, P. H. Pye-Smith, in an address to the British Association for the Advancement of Science in 1879.

With regard to the endowment of research in biology, I must
confess that I should be sorry to see it undertaken by government funds. That such investigations are of public interest,
that they are difficult and expensive, and that at present they
languish for want of adequate support, is all true . . . [but]
. . . Great as is the national importance of science, the nation
is more important still; and even if that were the alternative,
I would rather that we should indefinitely continue dependent
on Germany for our knowledge than give up the local energy,
the unofficial zeal which has made England what she is. Far
better for the strength and civilisation of the nation that a
thousand pounds were raised every year for the endowment
of unremunerative researches in this wealthy town of Sheffield
than that ten thousand were paid you by a paternal monarch
or an enlightened department.[93]

Such sentiments were echoed in Parliament whenever the subject
was broached.

Equally influential, perhaps, was the opinion referred to inci-
dentally by Lankester and early expressed in Parliament by
Samuelson: "The notion [in this country] that science is dreamy,
vague, untrustworthy, and useless to practical men."[94] In view of
the fact that the teaching of science as theoretical knowledge
exclusively had been the practice of the universities, and with but
two or three exceptions of other schools as well, to what other
conclusion could the practical men have come? In as much as
science instruction had been divided between the highest realm
of theoretical discovery and the simplest realm of techniques suitable to the artisan, as taught in the mechanics institutes or such
"polytechnics" as Quintin Hogg's in Regent Street, and because
of the low estate of the technologies in England, science had in
actual fact tended to be "dreamy and untrustworthy" for practical
ends. Only very slowly was this view of English science becoming
out-dated.

Despite the founding of the university colleges and the new
laboratories of the universities, the effect of the fear of German
commercial competition was principally to focus attention upon
the more immediately and discernibly profitable technical education. Technical education was popular with businessmen and poli-

ticians and salved the social consciences of the philanthropists. In terms of effort expended, probably the greatest advance made in the period was in the field of technical education, especially at the secondary school level.

As Playfair had begun the agitation in 1867 which led to the appointment of the Select Committee on Technical Education in 1868, so Mundella was instrumental in beginning the agitation which led to the Royal Commission on Technical Instruction in 1881.[95] He began by working through Philip Magnus. Magnus, upon returning from study at the University of Berlin, where he had learned to admire the German educational system, had been appointed Organising Director and Secretary of the City and Guilds Institute of London, a key position for the promotion of technical education.[96] The following year Mundella urged him to submit to the committee of the City and Guilds Institute for publication, a manuscript written by a friend, H. M. Felkin, living in Chemnitz. It was accepted and appeared in May of 1881 under the title of *Technical Education in a Saxon Town*. "What will strike everyone who carefully examines the figures contained in the following pages is the great cost of a well-organised system of technical instruction. . . ." wrote Magnus in the preface. "It remains to be seen whether, for the sake of increasing the industrial prosperity of this country, the people of England will be willing to make corresponding sacrifices."[97]

Mundella used the book to persuade the government to appoint a royal commission to make inquiries into the conditions of education in foreign countries, with special reference to its bearing on industrial pursuits.[98] Appointed to serve on the commission were: Bernhard Samuelson, as chairman, Henry Roscoe, Philip Magnus, John Slagg, Swire Smith, William Woodall, with Gilbert Redgrave as secretary.[99] The Royal Commission on Technical Instruction worked for three years, issuing a final report in three parts in 1884; one on American education by William Mather, another on agricultural instruction by Henry M. Jenkins, and the third on scientific instruction and trade schools on the Continent.[100] According to Magnus, the report "was widely circulated . . . and was for many years the recognised work of reference on all questions of technical education."[101] But the Commissioners did not permit the matter to rest there. "From 1884 onwards, during many years, the members of the Commission, more especially Sir Henry Roscoe, Sir Swire Smith, the late Mr. Woodall and myself," wrote Magnus, "addressed large meetings in nearly every manufacturing centre throughout the country."[102] Though other countries were not neglected, as had happened previously, Germany again played a stellar role in the report.[103]

An account of the advances made in technical education, much of which consisted of the founding of night schools for workers, often on the foundations of the old mechanics' institutes, and partly financed through the Science and Art Department, would take us far from our immediate interest. The most ambitious undertakings were the work of the City and Guilds Institute, founded for this purpose by the Livery Companies and similar guilds and by the Corporation of the City of London.[104] The first of their undertakings was the Finsbury Technical School, established in 1878 as a precursor to the Central Technical College, a teacher training technical school, founded in 1884.[105] Besides these, the Institute encouraged the founding of technical schools by donations, as in the founding in 1883 of the Manchester Technical School.[106] These institutions generally reflected the industrial interests of the local community.

A demand for commercial education, as well as for the more strictly technical, resulted from the Report of the Royal Commission on the Depression of Trade and Industry in 1885. The following year, when a proposal to establish an Imperial Institute was made in conjuncton with the celebration of the Jubilee year, the scientific, technical, and commercial interests came into conflict. Lockyer vigorously pressed the cause of the sciences as necessarily related to industry and in a leading article, "Science and the Jubilee," attacked the manner in which the project was being undertaken; he wanted the new institution to be "almost exclusively" scientific.[107] The next week he was able to hail the appointment of the chemist, Sir Frederick Abel, as the organizing secretary of the committee. The following week he returned to the subject, quoting an address Huxley had delivered at the Mansion House.

It was a hard thing to say, but the plain simple fact of the case was that industrial competition among the peoples of the world at the present time was warfare which must be carried on by the means of warfare. In what respect did modern warfare differ from ancient warfare? It differed because it had allied itself with science, because it trusted in knowledge, organised and disciplined . . . because it took advantage of every scientific discovery by which the weapons of offense and defense could be perfected . . . and if the peaceful warfare of industrialism was to succeed it must follow the same methods.[108]

A few weeks later, Abel addressed the Royal British Institution. After citing the Royal Commission on the Depression of Trade and Industry in connection with the deficiency of commercial as well as technical education, he continued:

The ordinary clerk in a merchant's office is too often made to feel his inferiority to his German colleague, not merely in regard to his lamentable deficiency in the knowledge of languages, but in respect to almost every branch of knowledge . . . The preliminary training for commercial life on the Continent is far more comprehensive, practical, and systematic than that which is attainable in this country, and the student of commerce abroad has, afterwards, opportunities for obtaining a high scientific and practical training.[109]

The address revealed, however, that those responsible for the new Institute were far from agreement with Lockyer, and shortly after, the editor lamented the indifference to science as signified by the fact that for the ceremony accompanying the laying of the cornerstone, no man of science, as such, was invited and that *Nature* had not received a press ticket.[110]

Meanwhile, mainly on the initiative of Roscoe and Huxley, a National Association for the Promotion of Technical Education was founded, and the Association sent an impressive delegation to urge supporting legislation from the government.[111] The result was the introduction in the Commons of a bill in 1887 for government assistance to technical education.

About the same time another demand for government aid was under way. For no sooner had the university colleges been founded than they discovered the difficulty of raising adequate funds from the local industrialists and philanthropists. In 1880 when William Ramsay, trained in chemistry at Glasgow and Tübingen, arrived at Bristol College to succeed Alfred Marshall, as principal, he discovered that both his assistants in chemistry were preparing to depart for study in Germany, and he experienced great difficulty in finding suitable successors. He could offer neither permanent appointments nor fixed salaries, the latter being customarily deducted from the professor's share of the student fees.[112] When the Welsh university colleges were voted an annual grant by Parliament in 1882, the hard-pressed principals of the English colleges united in an effort to secure similar government assistance.[113]

A leader of this movement, Ramsay recruited his forces from among those already active on behalf of education and technical training. Bristol College from its foundation had been aided financially by Balliol College and New College, Oxford, and Ramsay was brought into contact with Jowett. During a visit to Birmingham in December, 1886, staying with William Tilden of Mason's College, he had the opportunity of a long talk with Joseph Chamberlain. The result was a letter from Ramsay to the Lord Mayor, early in 1887, in which the contrast of the condition of higher education in Germany and in England furnished the theme.[114] By pre-arrangement Jowett sent a letter to the *Times*, followed by another from Roscoe, and supported by a leader in the *Times*. Mundella then opened the Parliamentary campaign. In Birmingham a public meeting was presided over by the Lord Mayor to which a supporting letter was sent by Joseph Chamberlain and the resolution read by the Reverend Dr. Robert Dale. In June a deputation, including Chamberlain, Sir John Lubbock, Mundella, Playfair, Samuelson, Tilden, Dr. Percival, and Sir George Young, was received by Goschen, Chancellor of the Exchequer.[115]

The campaign resulted in the recognition of the University Colleges as national institutions and the Parliamentary vote of an annual grant of £15,000 in 1889. As Ramsay's most recent biographer observes, this was the beginning of the "establishment of a number of independent universities, centres of research, and advanced teaching, which Ramsay with his knowledge of the German university system already clearly visualized."[116] With the passage in the same year of the Technical Education Act, largely due to the efforts of Goschen, "whose connections with Germany had opened his eyes to this country's deficiencies,"[117] technical instruction was finally recognized as an interest of the State, though no attempt was made to give it national direction. A year later Goschen was also responsible for providing funds for assistance to technical education through a tax on spirits and beer designed as a temperance measure.[118]

Despite these successes, the weakness of the movement for scientific and technical education was the same as that of every other movement for education in England in the nineteenth century: a great many schools were founded without systematic organization, and most of them were starved for funds because of the dissipation of both energy and money among such numbers.[119] But behind what was done, we find that much of the driving impulse was furnished by the German example and fear of German competition.

5.

Britain's backwardness

In the two decades preceding the Jubilee in 1887, the English had made real progress in scientific instruction under German influence. However, all informed scientists were in agreement that, despite the gains made, England was not even approaching equality with Germany. In 1883 Lankester made a carefully detailed examination of the funds, facilities, and offices available for the study of the biological sciences in Germany and England. "In proportion to its population (leaving aside the consideration of its greater wealth), England has," he concluded, "only about one-fourth of the provision for the advancement of biological research which exists in Germany." Estimating the financial expenditure necessary to bring England to an equality, he admitted that the proposal he was making "is gigantic and almost alarming in respect of the amount of money which it demands," adding that this "apparently extravagant and unheard of appropriation of public money *is actually made every year in Germany.*"[120]

In 1884 W. H. Perkin, one of England's most successful industrial chemists, delivered the presidential address to the Chemical Society. Perkin, former student of August von Hofmann, observed that for all the increase in facilities in England, original research was quantitatively no greater than in 1875. One reason for this was the inadequate instruction, especially in research, provided in England. Though English firms employed many fewer chemists than their German counterparts, even the few required had often to be recruited from abroad because of the insufficient training of the English students. The better English students of science still found it necessary to go abroad to receive really adequate schooling. In regard to the work which was being carried on in relation to chemistry, ". . . it may be thought by some that an undue weight has been given to that which is going on in Germany, and too little to that which is being carried on in this country; but I think if anyone will impartially compare one with the other, this will not be found to be the case . . . There is no doubt we do not hold the position we did as chemical manufacturers, and unless our chemical industries keep pace with chemical discovery fully as well as they do on the Continent, our position must further decline."[121] Perkin should have been well informed since two of his sons had recently studied in Germany.

When the Royal Commission on Technical Education issued its final report, once again the contrast between the continental, and more particularly the German, establishments were contrasted with the English, generally to the disadvantage of the latter. While something comparable, if less efficient and less well provided for, existed in England in continuation schools and universities, nothing was found to compare with the polytechnical higher schools of Germany. At no level of schooling was the quality of instruction offered in England believed to equal that in Germany. Again, too, the large financial outlay by the government in Germany—an outlay which brought educational costs within the reach of virtually every student—was stressed by the Commission and the very real need of the English colleges for funds was repeated.[122]

This report was apparently widely read, perhaps because of the return of the depression in trade. Coupled with the dismaying defection of England's leading industrial competitors from the "proven economic wisdom" of free trade by the erection of tariff walls, English businessmen and politicians were more receptive than at any time previously to the warnings of the scientists and educators. This was the background for Lyon Playfair's presidential address to the British Association at Aberdeen in 1885. Although he had been speaking to the same purpose since the days of Prince Albert, (whose address before the Association meeting in the same city in 1859 Playfair recalled), never before, according to Lockyer, had the subject "attracted at any one time the same earnest and general attention." Summarizing the reaction to the address in some fourteen newspapers and journals, Lockyer noted that only two or three rejected Playfair's claim that England was lagging in the sciences or were "not ashamed of the condition of scientific studies in England."[123]

Playfair defined his object as being "to point out how it is that science lags in its progress in the United Kingdom owing to the deficient interest taken in it by the middle and upper classes." The address was remarkable for its coverage of the principal subjects of relevance. Of the lack of government responsibility, he remarked that "All great countries except England have Ministers of Education, but this country has only ministers who are the managers of primary schools." Secondary education "is chaotic, and remains unconnected with the State." The universities "are still far from the attainment of a proper combination of their resources between teaching and research. Even Oxford and Cambridge, which have done so much in recent years in the equipment of laboratories and in adding to their scientific staff, are still far behind a second-class German university." Of the lack of technologists, he echoed Bulwer-Lytton's statement of fifty years earlier that "while England has never lacked leaders in science, they have too few followers to risk a rapid march. We might create an army to support our generals in science, as Germany has done . . . if education in this country would only mould itself to the needs of a scientific age." Of the effects felt in commerce, he inquired, "how is it that in our great commercial centres, foreigners—German, Swiss, Dutch, and even Greeks—push aside our English youth and take the places of profit? . . . How is it that in our colonies . . . German enterprise is pushing aside English incapacity? How is it that we find whole branches of manufactures, when they depend on scientific knowledge, passing away from this country? . . . The answer to these questions is that our systems of education are still too narrow for the increasing struggle for life." The sums spent by Prussia and other German states on their universities were relatively enormous by comparison to the aid given by the government of the United Kingdom. "Either all foreign States are strangely deceived in their belief that the competition of the world has become a competition of intellect, or we are marvelously unobservant of the change which is passing over Europe in the higher education of the people." "How unwise," he concluded, "it is for England to lag in the onward march of science when most other European Powers are using the resources of their States to promote higher education and to advance the boundaries of knowledge."[124]

The deficient interest of the middle and upper classes in England in the sciences and technologies can be partially attributed to simple ignorance, an ignorance which their education at the public schools or universities did little to dissipate. Similarly, British manufacturers clung to their old ways, only reluctantly employing technologists and clinging to the notion of apprenticeship in the shop as the only means of learning.[125] But the scientists were also Englishmen and too often shared the prejudices of their fellows even when they had the advantage of better education. Many of them appear to have been committed to training in pure science and opposed to technical training.[126] Most of them were as reluctant as other Englishmen to become professionalized.

An example of this appeared in the history of the Chemical Institute, one of many such organizations the new technological society was producing. With the passage of the Food and Drug Act in 1872, the demand for analytical chemists exceeded the supply. Official inspectors were recruited from men many of whom possessed only the most meager knowledge of chemistry. Fearing that the profession of chemist would fall into complete disrepute as a result of their errors and failures, a number of leading chemists, headed by Edward Frankland, founded the Institute of Chemistry. It differed from the Chemical Society in being a professional rather than a study society whose purpose was to fix standards of competence and to promote professional interests generally.[127]

After five years of steady increase in membership, a decline set in because of the seeming failure of the Institute to make any adequate return to the members for their dues. In 1885 the dues were reduced, and finally membership was thrown open to any who could produce satisfactory evidence of training and fitness without the examinations which had been previously required. The year, 1887, when the Institute received a royal charter, marked the beginning of a period of new and steady growth. But the crisis through which the Institute passed revealed the lack of any feeling of professional fellowship and pride among the members.[128]

This continued absence of a sense of professional solidarity among scientists generally was noted by Lockyer in connection with a dinner held in honor of John Tyndall in 1887.[129] Equally important was the indifference manifested toward science by the influential politicians and the Court. Of one of John Bright's speeches in which that great Liberal attributed England's prosperity wholly to free trade, Lockyer commented on his failure to take into account the contributions made by science and technology.[130]

Probably the most eloquent and distressed editorial that the founder of *Nature* ever penned appeared, like the later "Recessional," on the occasion of a Jubilee. Observing that the period of the Queen's reign was historically remarkable principally for the advances made in science and technology, he noted that what had been accomplished in England was done with only a bare minimum of assistance from the State. "It is a matter of fact, whatever the origin of the fact may be, that during the Queen's reign, since the death of the lamented Prince Consort, there has been an impassable gulf between the highest culture of the nation and Royalty itself. The brain of the nation has been divorced from the head." The lack of access of the leaders in literature, art, and science was, he believed, less detrimental to either the Queen or the notable men than to the State, since the impression it gave was that these render no service to the State. Abroad, these matters were differently ordered; men of letters, art, and science were welcomed into the councils of the Sovereign. "With us it is a matter of course that every Lord Mayor shall, and every President of the Royal Society shall not, be a member of the Privy Council; and a British Barnum may pass over a threshold which is denied to a Darwin, a Stokes, or a Huxley." Blaming the courtier class, who may have obtained literary culture at the universities, "but of science or of art . . . they are for the most part ignorant," he reported that in the arrangements for the Jubilee ceremonial in Westminister Abbey only one Fellow of the Royal Society, as such was invited, "while with regard to literature we believe not even this single exception has been made. It may be an excellent thing for men of science like Prof. Huxley, Prof. Adams, and Dr. Joule, and such a man of literature as Mr. Robert Browning, that they should not be required to attend at such a ceremonial, but it is bad for the ceremonial . . . Her Gracious Majesty suffers when a ceremonial is rendered not only ridiculous but contemptible by such mal-administration. England is not represented, but only England's paid officials and nobodies."[131]

For all of Lockyer's pessimism, and much of it was warranted, he and his associates had not worked wholly in vain. Ranked below the placemen, they had little success until almost the close of this period even in arousing the business community to some sense of the danger represented by better educated nations. Almost alone in Victorian England, these scientists, scholars, and their few industrialist allies recognized the implications of the modern technologies as these were being developed and exploited especially in Germany. Influenced by the Germans both in the positive form of admiring emulation and in the negative form of fear of economic rivalry, they tried year after year to awaken their compatriots to England's need for scientific instruction and for the reform and extension of education. Their success may be approximately measured by the advances made in English education in these two decades. Not the least important of these was the reform of Oxford and Cambridge Universities in the late seventies, to which subject we shall now turn.

Notes

CHAPTER III

1. See Ross J. Hoffman, *Great Britain and the German Trade Rivalry* (Philadelphia, Pa., 1933), esp. p. 20.

2. See Ch. V. of the complete manuscript.

3. Both letters are in the Fifth Report of the Commissioners for the Exhibition of 1851, Appendix O, *Parliamentary Papers* (1867), [3933], XXIII, 117–119.

4. *Ibid.*, 121–143. Two jurors either made no reply or their replies were not recorded. Cf. W. T. Jeans, *The Creators of the Age of Steel* (New York, 1884), pp. 256–260, who associates the founding of the Whitworth scholarships with this movement.

5. "Mundella, Anthony," *D. N. B.* See also W. H. G. Armytage, *A. J. Mundella, 1825–1897* (London, 1951).

6. 1867 [3933], 142.

7. "Samuelson, Bernhard," *D. N. B.*

8. Hansard, 3rd Series, CXCI (1867), 160.

9. *P. P.* 1867, LIV includes (137) Report of a Committee appointed by the Council of the British Association for the Advancement of Science, urging more scientific and technical instruction; (168) Answers from Chambers of Commerce to Queries of the Vice-President of the Council as to Technical Education; (13) Letter from B. Samuelson; (33) Report on Technical, Industrial, and Professional Instruction in Italy and other countries by Professor Leone Levi; [4085] Circular of Lord Stanley to her Majesty's Representatives Abroad, together with their replies. Armytage, *op. cit.*, pp. 51–52, has little on the Committee's origin, but is interesting on Mundella.

10. See Playfair's account, Hansard, 3rd Series, CSCVIII (1869), 204. See also a review of the Report, *Edinburgh Review*, CXXVII (1868), 433–468.

11. Matthew Arnold, *Schools and Universities on the Continent* (London, 1868), esp. pp. 278–281.

12. *Systematic Technical Education for the English People* (London, 1869). Phrase quoted from "Russell, J. Scott," *D. N. B.*

13. See D. L. Burn, "The Genesis of American Engineering Competition, 1850–1870," *Economic History*, II (1930–33), 296.

14. Hansard, 3rd Series, CXIX (1870), 465.

15. *Ibid.*, 477.

16. See T. Mary Lockyer and Winifred L. Lockyer with assistance of Prof. Herbert Dingle and Others, *Life and Work of Sir Norman Lockyer* (London, 1928), Ch. VI. Lockyer had a secondary school education and a year in Switzerland and France, but little or no training in the sciences.

17. O. J. Howarth, *The British Association for The Advancement of Science: A Retrospect 1831–1931* (London, 1931), Ch. I.

18. See A. M. Carr-Saunders and P. A. Wilson, *The Professions* (Oxford, 1933), p. 300.

19. The British Association was in this a notable exception, as was the Royal Society by this date, though the latter still had many non-scientific members. See H. Lyons, *The Royal Society 1660–1940* (Cambridge, 1944), Appendix II, p. 342, for the number of Fellows who were and were not scientists at various dates.

20. The Board of Education's Departmental Committee on the Royal College of Science in 1906 wrote that it was the "growing conviction that this country was falling behind in the race for industrial supremacy" that led to the appointment of this 1870 Commission. Final Report, 1906 [Cf. 2892], p. 5.

21. The Duke of Devonshire was Chancellor of Cambridge University and one-time President of Owens College, Manchester. Lubbock was a banker and entomologist. Stokes and Smith were professors of mathematics at Cambridge and Oxford, respectively. Miller was professor of chemistry at King's College, London, and a former student of Liebig. More will be said of Sharpey and Huxley presently.

22. The reports appeared as follows: First Report, 1871 [C. 318]; Second Report, 1872 [C. 536]; Third Report, 1873 [C. 868]; Fourth Report, 1874 [C. 884]; Fifth Report, 1874 [C. 1087]; Sixth Report, 1875 [C. 1279]; Seventh Report, 1875 [C. 1297]; Eighth Report, 1875 [C. 1298]. References will be made hereafter to the number of the report only.

23. First Report, pp. 101, 109.

24. See esp. the Sixth, Seventh, and Eighth Reports.

25. Eighth Report, p. 45.

26. *Nature*, XII (1875), 430.

27. Eighth Report, pp. 47–48; *Nature*, XII, 470.

28. See *Nature*, X (1874), 21–23, and XII (1875), 470.

29. *Nature*, XII, 361, 392.

30. *Nature*, II (1870), 449. For a still more explicit statement, see *Nature*, XXX (1884), 1–3.

31. General opinion was probably reflected by the reporter of the Schiller Anniversary Festival held in the Crystal Palace in 1859. "Germany was everywhere,—in the countenances, the talk, the behavior of the audience,—in the *insignia* of the gentlemen in office,— can we add, without ill nature, in the impractical bustle and gentle

confusion which marked the whole transaction." *The Athenaeum*, July-December, 1859, 639. Cf. *Collected Papers of Frederic William Maitland*, Ed. H. A. L. Fisher (Cambridge, 1911), III, p. 475.

32. See A. I. Tillyard, *A History of University Reform* (Cambridge, 1913) esp. p. 214; see also, Henry Sidgwick, "Idle Fellowships," *Contemporary Review*, 27 (1876), pp. 679–693.

33. Examples are numerous. See the evidence given by E. B. Pusey, 22 July 1867, regarding the London residence of the professor of civil law and the Lee's Reader for chemistry in the Special Report of the Select Committee on the Oxford and Cambridge Universities Education Bill, 1867 (497), 192. For a later instance, see Thomas Martin, *The Royal Institution* (London, 1942), p. 38.

34. As careful a statement as any is that of D. M. Winstanley, *Later Victorian Cambridge* (Cambridge, 1947), p. 331.

35. Tillyard, *op. cit.*, pp. 85, 217.

36. *The Times* (London), 20 November 1872, p. 4. Winstanley, *op. cit.*, p. 267, omits the words "and others" thus allowing the unwary reader to conclude that this was also a reform effort "from within." In part it was, but not exclusively.

37. See Mark Pattison, *Memoirs* (London, 1885), *passim*. Tillyard, *op. cit.*, pp. 162 ff. *Nature*, XIV (1876), 552.

38. Brodie had studied with Liebig at Giessen and greatly admired the German universities. See his testimony in *P. P.*, 1867 (497), XIII, 1–3. In 1867 in "Liberal Education in Universities," Seeley contrasted the encouragement of research and scholarship in the German universities with the failure in this respect of Oxford and Cambridge. See his *Roman Imperium and Other Essays* (Boston, 1871), pp. 198–202, 215, and 228–229.

39. *Nature*, VII (1872), 97–98.

40. *Nature*, XIV (1876), 398–99.

41. For 5 October 1878.

42. *Nature*, XVIII (1878), 610–614.

43. See Third Report, XV–XXVI.

44. Third Report, LIX; Seventh Report, 3.

45. See "Liberal Education in England," *Edinburgh Review*, CXXVII (1868), 131–165; Max Müller's description of the two old universities as "finishing schools for the well-to-do," was quoted approvingly by E. Ray Lankester, *Nature*, XIV (1876), 128.

46. See W. H. G. Armytage, *Civic Universities* (London, 1955), *passim*. Cf., M. E. Sadler, ed., *Continuation Schools in England and Elsewhere: Their Place in the Educational System of an Industrial and Commercial State* (Manchester, 1907), esp. p. 74. The *British Medical Journal*, 1883, II, 457–501, gives full information on their medical program, facilities, etc.

47. See the Second Report of the Commission on Technical Education, 1884 [C. 3981–III], 437.

48. *Nature*, I (1869), 157–159. Neither at Oxford nor Cambridge were there adequate facilities for a medical school. See Michael Foster, *On Medical Education at Cambridge* (London, 1878), p. 8, and "Medical Study at Oxford," by J. Burden-Sanderson, *Nature*, XXXIII (1886), 455–456.

49. *Nature*, I, (1869), 475–477.

50. *Nature*, I, 239.

51. Armytage, *op. cit.*, p. 224.

52. *Ibid.*, p. 227.

53. A more detailed account appears in Sir Thomas Edward Thorpe, *Sir Henry Roscoe* (London, 1916), pp. 53 ff.

54. Armytage, *op. cit.*, p. 223.

55. See J. A. Froude's letter, quoted in Herbert Paul, *The Life of Froude* (London, 1905), p. 224, written from Cornell University on the contrast between the English and American use of wealth.

56. *Nature*, XII (1875), 509. See also L. Playfair, *Nature*, XXXII (1885), 445; Thomas H. Huxley, "Introductory Address on University and Medical Training," *British Medical Journal*, 1874, II, 464–466, and "A Liberal Education" in *Science and Education* (New York, 1894), p. 97.

57. J. Reynolds Green, *A History of Botany in the United Kingdom from the Earliest Times to the end of the 19th-Century* (London, 1914), Ch. LIII.

58. A detailed survey of laboratory teaching facilities in the early eighties was made by the Royal Commission on Technical Education. See the Second Report, 1884 [C. 3981], Vol. I, Part III.

59. On the physiological and pathological laboratories, see *Nature*, XXXV (1886–87), 409–410.

60. *Nature*, II (1870), 449–450.

61. Maxwell's teaching began in 1872 but the laboratory was not open until 1874. Sir J. J. Thomson, "James Clerk Maxwell" in *James Clerk Maxwell: a Commemoration Volume* (Cambridge, 1931), mentions the names of ten laboratory students. In the same volume, Sir R. T. Glazebrook, "Early Days at the Cavendish Laboratory," names three others; and William Garnett, "Maxwell's Laboratory," three more. When J. H. Thomson took charge of the department in 1885, the number of research students, we are told, was "about ten," and this was after the five years during which Lord Rayleigh, much more of an experimentalist than Maxwell, had been in charge. See Alexander Wood, *The Cavendish Laboratory* (Cambridge, 1946), p. 30. However, 45 students were reported doing elementary work in the laboratory by the Commissioners on Technical Education in 1881. See their Second Report, Vol. I, p. 420.

62. The numbers and quotations are from "Some Memories" by Sir Ambrose Fleming in *James Clerk Maxwell*, p. 121. In the same volume

see Thomson, pp. 15–16; and Sir Horace Lamb, "Clerk Maxwell as Lecturer," p. 144. See also *Nature*, XII (1875), 204: "The magnificent laboratories of the Universities of Oxford and Cambridge and Dublin are nearly empty."

63. *Nature*, XXVIII (1883), 614.

64. Of the chemistry teachers in England during these two decades, the following, at least, were German-trained or studied under German-trained teachers: At Mason's College, W. A. Tilden (A. von Hofmann); Cambridge University, George D. Liveing (Rammelsberg); James Dewar (Playfair, Kékulé), Siegfried Ruhemann (A. von Hofmann); University College, Bristol, William Ramsey (Bunsen, Fittig); Cirencester Agricultural College, J. C. A. Voelcker (Liebig); Yorkshire College of Science, Leeds, T. E. Thorpe (Roscoe, Bunsen); King's College, London, William A. Miller (Liebig), C. L. Bloxam (A. von Hofmann), J. Millar Thomson (Playfair); University College, London, Alexander Williamson (Gmelin, Liebig); Central Technical College, London, Henry E. Armstrong (Frankland, Kolbe); Finsbury Technical College, Raphael Meldola (Frankland); Royal School of Mines, Edward A. Frankland (Bunsen, Liebig); Owens College, Manchester, Henry E. Roscoe (Bunsen), Carl Schorlemmer (Bunsen, H. Will, H. Kopp); Oxford University, B. C. Brodie (Liebig); Woolwich Military College, Frederick A. Abel (A. von Hofmann).

65. Matthew Arnold in his *Schools and Universities on the Continent* commented, pp. 278–279, that "in nothing do England and the Continent at the present moment more strikingly differ than in the prominence which is now given to the idea of science there, and the neglect in which this idea still lies here; a neglect so great that we hardly know the use of the word science in its strict sense, and only employ it in a secondary and incorrect sense." Cf., Sir Edward Sharpey-Schafer, "Development of Physiology," *Nature*, CIV (1919), 207–208.

66. J. Reynolds Green, *op. cit.*, p. 527.

67. Leonard Huxley, *Life and Letters of Thomas Henry Huxley* (New York, 1900), I, 112: "For the difference between this [Huxley's work] and the labours of the greatest English comparative anatomist of the time, whose detailed work was of the highest value, but whose generalization and speculations . . . proved barren and fruitless, lay in the fact that Huxley . . . had taken up the method of von Baer and Johannes Müller, then almost unknown, or at least unused in England." See also I, p. 9.

68. J. Reynolds Green, *op. cit.*, p. 528.

69. Sir Edward Sharpey-Schafer, *History of the Physiological Society during its First Fifty Years, 1876–1926* (London, 1927), p. 14.

70. *Ibid.*, p. 2.

71. *Ibid.*, pp. 22, 28.

72. *Ibid.*, p. 3 and n. 2. Trotter became Foster's principal supporter at Cambridge. See Foster's obituary notice on Trotter in *Nature*, XXXVII (1887), 153–154.

73. Huxley, *op. cit.*, I, 406–407; Green, *op. cit.*, p. 528; F. O. Bower, *Sixty Years of Botany in Britain (1875–1935)* (London, 1938), pp. 45–46.

74. Huxley, *op. cit.*, I, note to p. 406.

75. J. Reynolds Green, *op. cit.*, pp. 528 ff.

76. Among them were Lauder Brunton, William Rutherford, H. N. Moseley, E. Ray Lankester, William Stirling, W. H. Gaskell, J. T. Cash, Meade Smith, L. C. Wooldridge, C. E. Beevor, G. A. Buckmaster, W. H. Thompson, Vaughan Harley, and Arthur Gamgee. See William Stirling, "In Memoriam—Karl Ludwig," *The Medical Chronicle*, Manchester, N. S. III (Apr.-Sept., 1895), 178–191; and "Gamgee, Arthur," *D. N. B.*

77. Sharpey-Schafer, *op. cit.*, pp. 24–25.

78. Among the Cambridge men, Newell Martin's career took him to the Johns Hopkins University; Francis Balfour, who worked with Dohrn at Naples, died at the outset of a Cambridge professorship; W. H. Gaskell and J. N. Langley remained at Cambridge, the latter succeeding Foster; C. T. Roy studied in Berlin, Strasbourg and Leipzig before becoming professor of pathology at Cambridge; Henry Head went to Liverpool, and Charles Sherrington to Oxford.

79. "Lankester, Edwin Ray," *D. N. B.*

80. Quoted by J. Reynolds Green, *op. cit.*, pp. 530–532.

81. Among others were Sydney Vines, Bailey Balfour, Francis Darwin, H. M. Ward, F. O. Bower, W. R. McNab, Walter Gardiner, and D. H. Scott. See Green, *op. cit.*, pp. 531 ff., and Bower, *op. cit.*, pp. 48 ff.

82. J. Reynolds Green, *op. cit.*, pp. 531 ff.; Bower, *op. cit.*, pp. 48 ff. D. H. Scott, famous paleobotanist, went to Waltzburg on Thiselton-Dyer's advice. Scott lectured at University College, London, before becoming Honorary Keeper of the Jodrell Laboratory in 1892, in Obit. Notices of the Fellows of the Royal Society, I, 1930–35, pp. 205–227.

83. Of Vines' students, Harry Marshall Ward succeeded Babbington in the chair at Cambridge; Bower went to Glasgow; Phillips, to Bangor; Percival, to Wye and Reading; Oliver, to University College, London; Groom, to the Imperial College of Science; Green, to Liverpool. Of Darwin's students, Burhill went to Singapore; Willis, to Ceylon; Pearson, to Capetown; Bottomley, to King's College, London. Biffen held a post at Cambridge; Yapp went to Aberystwyth; Vaughan, to Belfast; and Blackman, to the Imperial College of Science. See Green, *passim.*

84. *Nature*, XVIII (1878), 611; XXV (1881), 25–26; XXXII (1885), 193.

85. J. Reynolds Green, *op. cit.*, p. 534; Bower, *op. cit.*, p. 53.

86. J. Reynolds Green, *op. cit.*, p. 54.

87. *Ibid.*, p. 546; Bower, *op. cit.*, pp. 29–30.

88. Sharpey-Schafer, *op. cit.*, pp. 26–27.

89. Bower, *op. cit.*, pp. 60–64. I. Bailey Balfour graduated from Edinburgh, studied with von Sachs and de Bary, assisted both Huxley and Lister. He was successively professor of botany at Glasgow, Oxford, and Edinburgh, reforming the study at all three universities. See Bower, Ch. III, and Green, *op. cit.*, p. 547.

90. Sharpey-Schafer, *op. cit.*, pp. 5 ff. Of the nineteen men listed as the first movers of the Society, eight had studied in Germany: William Sharpey, G. H. Lewes, Brunton, Pye-Smith, Gaskell, E. E. Klein, F. Darwin, and G. F. Yeo. Michael Foster and Foster's students, John Marshall and Sharpey-Schafer, were strongly influenced by German concepts and practice. Two others, Pavy and Burdon-Sanderson, had, as already noted, studied in France.

91. See *Nature*, XXX (1884), 25, 40, 123, 350–351; XXXIV (1886), 177–181; XXXVIII (1888), 198–201, 236–237.

92. Hoffman, *op. cit.*, pp. 28 ff.

93. *Nature*, XX (1879), 408–413. Pye-Smith had himself studied both in Vienna and Berlin. This represents the sole expression of such opinion by a trained scientist that I have found, though, of course, there may have been others.

94. E. Ray Lankester, *The Advancement of Science* (London, 1890), p. 199.

95. Something of the reason for it is revealed in a statement Mundella made in the Commons. "I had seen what Germany was doing 20 years before [last autumn]; but I must confess that I was perfectly astounded at the development which has been made in the last seven or ten years. My hon. Friend . . . spoke of an institution [in England] which is to cost £20,000 to £30,000 to build. There are institutions which have been established within the last four years abroad which have cost as much as £100,000, compared with which there is nothing at all in this country." Hansard, 3rd Series, CCLX (1880), 539.

96. Philip Magnus, *Educational Aims and Efforts, 1880–1910* (London, 1910), pp. 14, 50, 51.

97. *Ibid.*, p. 91.

98. *Ibid.*, p. 92; Hansard, 3rd Series, CCLX (1880), 527–548.

99. Samuelson represented iron and machinery; John Slagg, cotton; Smith, wool; Roscoe, chemicals; Woodall, pottery; Magnus, technical education; and Redgrave, the science and art department. See Sir Swire Smith, *The Real German Rivalry* (London, 1916), pp. 23 ff. Also, Armytage, *Mundella*, p. 209.

100. The Commission's reports appeared in 1882 and 1884. The one of particular interest here is the Second Report, Vol. I, in *P. P.*, 1884 [C. 3981], XXIX.

101. Magnus, *op. cit.*, p. 94.

102. *Ibid.*, pp. 94–95, lists 39 towns in which he alone spoke; Cf. Thorpe, *op. cit.*, pp. 152–153.

103. See the summary of the report in *Nature*, XXX (1884), 113–114.

104. Magnus, *op. cit.*, p. 85; and C. T. Millis, *Technical Education* (London, 1925), pp. 53 ff. See also S. J. Curtis, *History of Education in Great Britain* (London, 1953), pp. 481 ff.

105. Magnus, *op. cit.*, pp. 87, 97; Millis, *op. cit.*, p. 61; *Nature*, XXIV (1881), 262–263.

106. Magnus, *op. cit.*, p. 231 and note; Millis, *op. cit.*, pp. 67 ff.

107. *Nature*, XXXV (1886–87), 217–218.

108. *Nature*, XXXV, 265–266. Mundella was also active. See Armytage, *op. cit.*, p. 270.

109. *Nature*, XXXVI (1887), 19.

110. *Nature*, XXXVI, 229.

111. Magnus, *op. cit.*, p. 111; *Nature*, XXXVI, 229–230; Armytage, *op. cit.*, pp. 270–271.

112. Morris W. Travers, *Life of Sir William Ramsay* (London, 1956), p. 46.

113. William A. Tilden, *Sir William Ramsey: Memorials of his Life and Work* (London, 1918), pp. 90–92.

114. Travers, *op. cit.*, pp. 75–77.

115. Tilden, *op. cit.*, pp. 93–99.

116. Travers, *op. cit.*, pp. 79–80.

117. Williams Gibbons and Reginald W. Bell, *History of the London County Council, 1889–1939* (London, 1939), p. 244.

118. *Ibid.*, p. 245.

119. In *Nature*, XXXIII (1885), 491–492, T. E. Thorpe wrote concerning technical education: "We have as yet no system. That is, of course, characteristic of us . . . Nothing in our whole educational history is more characteristic of us—of our energy, public spirit, and independence—than the way in which with much effort, laborious and occasionally ill-directed, and with no inconsiderable expenditure of money, we are hammering away at this question of teaching technology. In Yorkshire alone there is at the present moment probably every type of technical school more or less imperfectly developed, which the ingenuity or perversity of man could devise."

120. *Nature*, XXVIII (1883), 517 ff., esp. 520–523. Emphasis in original. More briefly reported in the *British Medical Journal*, 1883, II, 646, it was collected under the title, "Biology and the State," in his *Advancement of Science*, pp. 63–117.

121. *Nature*, XXX (1884), 246–248. Cf., Henry E. Armstrong's address to the British Association at Aberdeen in *Nature*, XXXII (1885), 453.

122. See the Second Report, and *Nature*, XXX (1884), 112–113.

Smith, p. 25, was to recall later: "I must here mention the visit of the Commissioners to the chemical laboratory of the University of Munich. We saw in this laboratory, one of very many in Germany, more students taking up research and the high branches of chemistry than could have been found in all the Universities and Colleges in England put together."

123. *Nature*, XXXII (1885), 497–499.

124. *Ibid.*, 438–446.

125. See Mundella's remarks in Hansard, 3rd Series, CCLX (1880), 538.

126. See for example Alexander Williamson's testimony before the Devonshire Commission.

127. The Institute of Chemistry . . . , *History of the Institute: 1877–1914*, compiled by Richard B. Pilcher (London, 1914), pp. 23–24. Cf., Carr-Saunders and Wilson, *op. cit.*, pp. 167–169.

128. *Ibid.*, pp. 80–88. See also *Chemical News and Journal of Industrial Science*, LI (1885), 127–129.

129. *Nature*, XXXVI (1887), 217–218.

130. *Nature*, XXI (1879–80), 296.

131. *Nature*, XXXVI (1887), 145–146.

The Second Reform of the Universities of Cambridge and Oxford

Reform of the Universities of Cambridge and Oxford in the late seventies, insofar as it resulted from internal pressures, was a consequence of the increased interest in specialized studies. In the collegiate scheme, there was little place for them, whether they were physical or biological sciences or the new humanistic "sciences." Collegiate education was based on an acquaintance with a limited number of books or a syllabus covering a few broad areas of study. The object was to train for general intelligence. But specialized studies, based on the mastery of a limited subject-matter and calling for further exploration and investigation, were predicated on the assumption of a life-long professional interest. The concern for specialization turned the reformers' interest away from the colleges to focus upon the university as the administrative center. But the universities, apart from the endowments for professorships, lacked funds to provide for laboratories, museums, libraries, and personnel. Managed largely by leading college officials, they were also usually indifferent to needs not pertaining to the colleges.

The question of introducing special subjects had been broached in various forms before the university commissions in the fifties but besides requiring professional lectures and the introduction of honors school or tripos in history and law and in natural philosophy, little was done. And the professional lectures existed, as Stubbs discovered, only on sufferance. Dissatisfaction with this situation arose concomitantly with the increasing secularism which undermined the position of the college fellows.[1]

As Augustus Leigh of King's College, Cambridge, observed, life fellowships and celibacy went together.[2] Similarly as clerical life lost its attraction, the position of the tutors underwent serious alteration. Jowett clearly described their predicament. "Formerly, a college tutor was a clergyman; if he was able and ambitious he looked to preferment in the Church, and if he was not, he went off upon a college living. That has so far passed away, that it is absolutely necessary to find some kind of career to which a college tutor can look forward."[3] Apart from the question of financial support, what sort of career was this to be? Once asked, the answer was supplied by the Germanists: that of the scholar-teacher, a man who, instead of spending a few years waiting for a college living by tutoring, planned to make a professional career out of study and teaching.[4] The new profession of the scholar-teacher emerged with the secularization of studies in the English universities, and the introduction of specialization and the publication of scholarly works as the road to distinction and promotion.

A few men in the universities had the worthy but limited objective of enabling more of their students to enter the civil service by improving instruction in their colleges.[5] But this was important only in those colleges which had largely ignored the earlier reform; it was not the basic problem leading to reform in the seventies. More pressing were the needs and demands of the scientist and the professional scholars.

By the seventies three groups interested in reform could be distinguished within the universities, and all three had been strongly influenced by the Germans: the experimental scientists, the philosophic idealists, and those who may be called the professional scholars. The philosophic idealists wished to reconstruct the English universities into more efficient educational institutions so they might be more useful to the State. The professional scholars wished to introduce the institutional methods of the Germans; secular in their interests, they championed the cause of pure scholarship and research. To them it seemed that the advancement of learning and the training of specialists was the function of a university and would contribute more to the welfare of the state than would a general, but necessarily more superficial, education for a larger number of students. Though willing, and even anxious, as were the philosophic idealists, to enable intellectually able men of all classes to come to the universities, the professional scholars wished also to raise the intellectual standards of university work by abolishing pass work and limiting the degree to honors students. In general the experimental scientists, especially those who had themselves been influenced by the Germans, supported this group.

Difficult as it often is to draw the line between the two groups, the division was of great importance. It was, for example, more important than the division between the humanities and the sciences, which occasioned little controversy in the reform; it was more important because it posed the educational dilemma of all modern democratic states.

This dilemma stemmed from the conflict between the need and demand of a liberal democracy for an education which would enable men to think and to exercise judgment for themselves as individuals and citizens; and the growing need of the state for professionally and technically trained men, requiring a more specialized education. It was the dilemma of liberal versus technological education. This dilemma was not to remain peculiar to Britain; it would in time become common to all democratic states. But it became critical for Britain early because of the challenge posed by Germany. The new German Empire offered competition in power and in all that contributed to power in the modern world: in education, in science, in technology, in industry and trade, in imperial aggressiveness and in· the capacity to wage war. This competition precipitated the crisis in Great Britain, which Prince Albert and a few scientists and scholars had, however vaguely, long forseen.

1.

Two plans of reform: Jowett's and Pattison's

The real struggle in the universities in the seventies might be described as a struggle between the older German ideal of *Bildung* and the ideal of *Wissenschaft*, of the study of the humanities and the sciences as a means to forming a cultivated mind and spirit as contrasted with both the humanities and the sciences pursued as specialized and positivist disciplines for the sake of increased knowledge.[6] Those men for whom Jowett may be taken as spokesman had usually been more influenced by German philosophic thought or by German conceptual schemes in the individual subjects. The professional scholars, led by Mark Pattison, though often influenced by German concepts, were more eager to adopt the methods pursued by the Germans, especially in laboratory experiment and original research, and to follow their institutional lead. Through the former, the German influence advanced the cause of education in England generally; through the latter, that influence advanced the cause of scientific scholarship and research.

Before the Oxford University Commission of 1850 Jowett had urged more scholarly activity at Oxford. This was at the time of his deepest engagement with German philosophy and his closest acquaintance with German scholars. But after his work with George Trevelyan and Macaulay for the civil service, and after the attack on him resulting from his studies in religion, the emphasis in his thinking in education moved continuously toward broadening the scope of education and extending it to include a greater number of the able men of the country in the interest of the state.

The effort to develop research and professional scholarship in the universities was taken up by Mark Pattison who, after his testimony before the Commission of the fifties, did a more decided about-face than Jowett and in the reverse direction. In the late fifties Pattison spent some time in Germany to study German education for the Newcastle Commission. His report made it clear that he was not an uncritical admirer of the German system. He saw, as many of his followers did not, and as he himself seems often to have forgotten, the consequences of specialization: the specialist's frequent ignorance of, and indifference to everything falling outside his area of expert competence, including public affairs. What he found to admire, however, in the German universities was what he believed his young disciple, Charles Appleton, found at Heidelberg and Berlin in 1865–66. Of him, Pattison wrote that what he really brought back from Germany

> "was the only thing of value which a German university has to offer—viz., the scientific spirit . . . Once awakened to this

perception, he became aware that a country or a university which is without this spirit is without the most powerful instrument of mental training. The return to his own university made him feel more keenly still by contrast the absence of any real educative power in her teaching.[7]

This "scientific spirit," a faith in *Wissenschaft*, gave many of the Englishmen going to Germany a new understanding not only of the importance of specialized study but also of the meaning of original research based on a systematic knowledge of what had gone before. In turn, this placed a new value on systematic organization in education, since its object was now taken to be the mastery of a "scientific" discipline. Returning from the German universities with the specialist's or professional's conception of knowledge, English scholars made "research" a symbol, and the natural and physical scientists made "laboratory experiment" a symbol. In the name of these symbols they demanded reform of their own universities.[8]

Both Jowett and Pattison were concerned that the English universities should contribute to the well-being of the nation and state and not function merely as appendages of the Church. Both recognized that Cambridge and Oxford were class institutions and wished to throw them open to men of all classes. Pattison insisted that the existing exhibitions and scholarships were really bounties paid to force impecunious students to accept the kind of education the universities offered and could at best affect but a small handful. "There is no reason," he wrote, "why every class of vocation in which intelligence and refinement are applicable . . . should not have a corresponding 'Faculty' arranged for it in the University, where an appropriate training—not practical and professional but theoretical and scientific—might be had. Why should commerce and industry choose to remain under the stigma which the feudal system branded upon them, as base employments, which necessarily excluded from the education which was reserved for the territorial seigneur and the cleric?"[9] Jowett urged reduction of the expense of university education by the admission of 'unattached' students, who could live outside the colleges as cheaply as they cared. And in 1874 he urged the founding of polytechnical colleges in all the great industrial centers. Both men urged a graded professoriate and were in agreement on many other matters.

One essential difference remained, however. Jowett was predominantly interested in what Pattison with considerable disdain labelled "education." The distinction which the latter wished to make appears in the following statement. "In proposing the German University as the model to which we must look in making any alterations in our own, I wish to confine myself entirely to this single point of view—viz. of a central association of men of science . . . What I wish to contend is, that the Professor of a modern University ought to regard himself primarily as a learner, and a teacher only secondarily. His first obligation is to the Faculty he represents; he must consider that he is there on his own account, and not for the sake of his pupils."[10] Jowett, on the contrary, placed less emphasis upon the professoriate, as scholars dedicated to research or to their special faculty, and more upon their teaching duties.[11] Pattison frankly wanted to model university instruction largely on the German professorial system; Jowett wanted to equal Germany in learning and scholarship by strengthening national education at all levels, including that in the old universities. He wanted the universities to become more efficient as national institutions of both teaching and learning, while retaining, on the whole, the English pattern with its careful direction of the students' program of studies and individual supervision. He further wished to extend the faculties, broaden the curriculum, and open the universities to all men of ability regardless of class. The differences in their views were not just the differences of two minds. Though Pattison found in scholarship and writing a haven from the trials of society, and Jowett found in scholarship and teaching an open sesame to society and success in the world, the difference of emphasis in educational ideals represented the developing conflict between two educational concepts, a conflict both suggested by German example and sharpened by German rivalry.

These two groups found common cause, however, in dissatisfaction with the condition of the Universities after the limited reforms made in the fifties, and they worked together against the university conservatives. Pattison and his group and Jowett and his followers were, with the scientists, largely responsible for the movement within the universities which, under pressure of attacks from without, culminated in the Parliamentary reform of the seventies.

Their dissatisfaction was brought into focus in the years after 1866 when it coincided with events and opinion in the world outside university walls. The shock of Prussia's quick victory over Austria in 1866, the even more astonishing German conquest of France in 1870–71, the Continental triumphs in the Paris International Exhibition, and the Parliamentary Reform of 1867, all combined to give an enormous impetus to the concern for education evidenced by three publications in 1868: Pattison's *Suggestions on Academical Organization, with Especial Reference to Oxford*, Goldwin Smith's *Reorganization of the University of Oxford*, and Matthew Arnold's *Schools and Universities on the Continent*. Arnold seriously warned of the necessity of reform to keep pace with Germany. In 1867 a Select Committee of the Commons was studying the universities of Cambridge and Oxford; in 1868 a Select Committee was appointed to investigate technical education abroad, and the Taunton Commission reported on secondary education. In 1870, W. E. Forster introduced his Education Bill; a Select Committee of the Lords was taking evidence for the University Test Bill which resulted in the abolition of religious tests for degrees at Oxford and Cambridge, and the Devonshire Commission was appointed to investigate scientific instruction. In 1872 the Cleveland Commission was appointed to investigate the financial affairs of the two ancient universities. The ferment of educational reform was remarkable.[12] Behind it lay the middle class and Dissenter demand for national education and admission to the old universities; behind it lay the technical advances made in the United States, as well as the high achievements of the German universities and the threat of the German trade rivalry.

The Select Committee of the Commons in 1867 was seeking to determine how the ancient universities might be opened to larger numbers. In moving the second reading of the bill which preceded its appointment, William Ewart, who was to serve as chairman of the committee, defined its objective: "to open the Universities to students without obliging them to be members of any College in

those Universities—in fact, to restore the ancient University system, as now practiced in Germany and Scotland . . ."[13] After
citing instances of unproductive professional sinecures at Cambridge and Oxford, he exclaimed: "Meantime, what strides have
been made under the professional system, by the great intellect of
Germany! All our deeper books in grammar, history, science, and
theology come from thence."[14] Jowett's close friend, Robert Lowe,
strongly supported the proposal,[15] as did Gladstone, who cited
the continuing decline in the proportion of the professional men,
clergymen, barristers, and physicians, who received any part of
their education at Oxford or Cambridge.[16] Beresford Hope, High
Church member for Cambridge, who had been opposing educational reform on the German model in Parliament for over a
decade,[17] raised the most violent objection, attacking any comparison of the English universities with the Scottish or German,
and asserting that it would be a grave mistake to introduce the
social system of the German students.[18]

The committee was appointed and after hearing much contra-
dictory testimony, called Jowett as witness. Supporting the proposal for unattached students, he must have brought a sense of
authority and freshness into the hearings for his evidence was by
all odds the longest. Having noted that the two universities drew
students only from "what may roughly be called the upper hundred
thousand at the most" and that men of ability should be drawn
from all classes, he was challenged by Beresford Hope, who sought
to force an admission that men of the lower social classes did not
have adequate educational preparation nor, on the average, the
necessary ability to profit by study at the universities. "I said,"
Jowett finally replied, "that there was no limit I could place to
persons of exceptional ability finding their way up if you gave
them the necessary helps of early education . . ."[19] And when the
same questioner, having elicited from him an admission that the
development of London University and the new collegiate schools
in the towns were antagonistic to the extension of education by
Oxford and Cambridge, asked: "As a very distinguished member
of one of our old Universities, do you look upon that phenomenon
with misgiving or the contrary?" he received the magnificent reply:
"I do not look upon any extension of education with anything

like misgiving. I think it probable that there are advantages which the old Universities possess which those colleges have not. There is a larger world and perhaps better teaching in them. I do not know sufficiently of those colleges to speak in detail about them; but I should wish them to flourish, and I should wish, at the same time, that more of their members were brought up to the old Universities."[20]

Another member of the Committee was Mountstuart Elphinstone Grant Duff, a Baliol man, a friend of Jowett and a closer friend of Mark Pattison and others among the professional scholars.[21] That he had been well-tutored by his friends became clear when, under his questioning, comparison was made of the Scottish and German universities with Oxford. Questioning W. L. Newman, history lecturer of Balliol, he asked: "Have you ever considered why Oxford does so little for classical learning when compared with the Universities of Germany?" and followed by inquiring: "You would say, would you not, that the German Universities have in our time done more for historical learning, not only than all other Universities put together, but more than all persons or bodies whatsoever, independently of the Universities, within the last 40 years?" "I think," was the reply, "that that is quite a tenable view."[22]

When Jowett was recalled a second day, Grant Duff began the questioning by leading him to state the desirability of an increase in the professors and an expansion of their role in teaching. The questioning then proceeded as follows.

> At present a young man going to the University of Berlin or Heidelberg, would have quite different opportunities of becoming an accomplished theologian, would he not, from what he would have at Oxford?—Yes, he would.
>
> Would he not find a far greater number of professors?—Yes.
>
> And he would have a regular course through which he would be expected to go?—Yes.[23]

Similar questions with similar replies continued through a variety of disciplines, vividly illustrating the insufficiencies of Oxford by the contrast.

When the old enemy of University reform, E. B. Pusey, was called to testify, he attacked the idea of having students unattached to the colleges on the grounds that their moral life could not be adequately supervised and declared that morality was very lax at the Scottish and German universities. Under severe questioning by Grant Duff, he admitted that his knowledge of the German universities was limited to the 1820's. Bluntly asked why German universities produced all the important works of scholarship, he attempted to deny it by citing eighteenth and early nineteenth century English works of scholarship. But the only works of recent date to which he could refer were Gaisford's *Poetae Minores* and Liddell's *Lexicon*.[24]

More pertinent was his defense of catechetical as opposed to professorial teaching. He argued that, without discussion, young men, while lacking intellectual defenses, were exposed to whatever doctrines the professor presented. This resulted in a training in doctrines rather than in a training of the mind. The consequence was a competition among schools of thought in Germany such as did not exist in England. But any value his argument had as a defense of liberal education was nullified by being carried to absurd extremes.[25]

If any members of the Committee lacked knowledge of the German universities, they received an ample education from the last witness, Dr. Walter Copland Perry, a doctor of philosophy of the University of Göttingen, a member of the English bar, and for twenty years, as a resident of Bonn, in intimate contact with its university. His admiration for the German institution was unstinted. He contradicted Pusey's charge of immorality on the part of the students, and under questioning by Grant Duff, put into the record the syllabus of lectures delivered at the University of Berlin in 1844 which, he asserted, was representative of the current year also. His testimony was second in length only to Jowett's.[26]

Asked about the opinion held of English scholars and scholarship by the Germans, he declared that the English were highly respected. Richard Bentley was one of their heroes. And although they believed that English scholars had much learning, they were surprised by the paucity of productive scholarship in England.

About the same time, James M. Hart, one of many Americans studying in Germany, wrote:

> Regarding science and scholarship in the aggregate, then, I venture to assert that there are only two departments in which the English are at the present time prominent, viz., pure mathematics and natural history. In all the others, they play a subordinate part. And in these two departments themselves, the universities have but a small share.[27]

And he proceeded through a long list of studies in which he found the Germans to be leaders.

Against this may be set the laudatory account of Cambridge by another American. Enjoying the life of an undergraduate, Charles Astor Bristed surrendered to the charm of the place and found plenty of work to do.[28] But it does not seem to have occurred to him to inquire if his learned masters were world authorities. Nor would it have occurred, one is sure, to the majority of the English dons themselves. Had the latter heard from the German-schooled American that they were "laggards in the great international handicap," they would simply have denied that they were entered in any such race or that such a thing existed in the world of scholarship. Many of them were well-read, even, after the English fashion, learned men. All of this was understood at the high tables and in the common rooms. Such knowledge as they had would also be properly passed on through conversation with those men who were worthy and interested enough to receive it. To publish for a larger audience, besides seeming a bit pretentious and laying the authors open to public criticism,[29] hardly seemed worthwhile. For where was the audience? Certainly not in England, where Stubbs was sure an historical journal would not pay,[30] and scholarly journals of any sort were rare. Not in England—and that was all their thought. That was the reason an intelligent American could describe the two English Universities as provincial literary coteries rather than centers of the universe of knowledge.[31]

Reviewing Stubbs' inaugural address in 1867, J. R. Green observed: "Mr. Stubbs will have done a real service to Oxford if only by reminding her that her work must ever be estimated by her relation to the world of letters and education of which she is but a part."[32] In its insularity the intramural world was an accurate reflection of the extramural world of England. Yet even as Green wrote, this was beginning to be changed, and it was the Germans, as no others, who were compelling Englishmen to recognize certain disadvantages resulting from their insularity.

2.

Recognition of the "majesty of German knowledge"

The same year that the Select Committee sat, Charles Appleton, just returned from Germany, published a translation of a pamphlet, *Universities Past and Present* by Dr. Johann Doellinger of Munich,[33] as his opening effort in support of university research. In 1869 he founded and began his editorship of the *Academy*, a journal intended to present, review, and encourage scholarly research in England. Founded on the model of the German journal, *Literarisches Centralblatt für Deutschland*, he marshalled in its support his Oxford friends who were trained or interested in German scholarship.[34]

But his activities were not confined to this undertaking. In 1872 he attempted to found an association for the support and promotion of "nature study and scientific research." This was the group, already referred to, at whose first meeting Mark Pattison presided in London.[35] The association lasted for two meetings only, breaking up in disagreement, due apparently to the fear of the utilitarians that idleness rather than research would be endowed, a reasonable enough fear considering the state of Oxford and Cambridge in that day.[36]

When Parliament began to consider the reform of the two old universities, Appleton put together a series of essays on the *Endowment of Research*, for which he persuaded Mark Pattison to write an introductory essay.[37] In addition to Pattison and Appleton, the latter represented by two previously published essays, the contributors were James S. Cotton, A. H. Sayce, Henry Clifton Sorby, Thomas K. Cheyne, Thistleton-Dyer, and Henry Nettleship. Except for the scientists, Sorby and Thistleton-Dyer, they were all concerned with the need of the universities for funds, as against the colleges, for the purpose of forwarding research in the humanistic studies, and all frequently cited Germany in urging the desirability of original work as opposed to the examination system.[38]

The Devonshire Commission issued a report on the two universities in 1873,[39] Jowett set forth "Suggestions for University Reform, 1874," and the Cleveland Commission issued also in 1874 its report on the finances of the Universities and the Colleges. Upon the request of the government, the Hebdomadal Council at Oxford and a Syndicate at Cambridge drew up suggestions of the needs of the universities.[40] By the time that was completed, however, the Liberal government had been defeated at the polls.

Despite the expectation of many Liberals that nothing more would be heard of university reform, the Conservative government in 1876 surprised them by proposing to appoint an executive Parliamentary commission, instead of another commission of investigation, to carry through such reforms of the University of Oxford as the various commissions had shown to be desirable.[41] That the Conservatives sought to make merely a gesture is improbable, though the bill was introduced so late in the session as to make action upon it unlikely. Rather it seems that the thinking of the Conservatives was undergoing some change; their interests by the mid-seventies were more secular, nationalist, and imperialist. Feeling that university reform was inevitable, they preferred to keep it in their own hands, while reaping any political reward which might accrue from it.[42]

The purposes of a commission on the University of Oxford were set forth in the House of Lords by Salisbury, and in the Commons, by Gathorne Hardy. The work of the Commissions of 1850 had been excellent. Since then two Commissions, one on scientific instruction and one on the revenues of the Universities had reported. The latter revealed that the average income per undergraduate in all the Colleges was £203. But great variations existed among the Colleges: in Exeter only £97, in Trinity only £96, in Balliol £75 was spent per student. If education were provided as cheaply in all the Colleges as in these, an annual saving of £165,578 to £197,700 could be effected. Where did this money presently go? "The real gist of the whole question," declared Lord Salisbury, "lies in the Fellowships and in the giving men £250 and £300 a year without any duties attached to the

Fellowships . . . They are, no doubt, given for success in certain examinations; but these are not of a remarkably high order . . ." The Commission should then regard the recommendations of the Hebdomadal Council as an indication of requirements. New buildings, museums, laboratories were needed, and new professorships or lectureships. Academic salaries, especially for the professors, needed improving. The Devonshire Commission had recommended more scientific research.[43]

The Duke of Devonshire himself promptly seconded the proposal, expressing the hope that the same might be done for Cambridge within the year. There the Colleges "already possessed considerable power" but looking to the past, he could not conceal from himself that it was desirable that a little external pressure should be brought to bear upon the Universities, and that it would not do to trust either the Universities or the Colleges with the entire management of the reform.[44] The same sense that reform from within was unlikely to achieve his intention was implicit in Salisbury's proposal to give this commission greater powers than that of 1854 because the latter had had for its object the reorganization of the wealth of the Colleges for the benefit of the Colleges themselves; but the object of the present bill was to apply the revenues of the Colleges "not to the interest of the Colleges, but to the interests of the University." It was "for the interest alike of the students and of the nation at large" that the reforms were to be made.[45]

The Liberals and a number of university reformers, partly for party reasons, partly for fear of the kind of reform Conservatives were thought likely to sponsor, on the whole opposed the appointment of an executive commission. So vague were the purposes outlined and so extensive the Commission's power, that some saw an intention to reverse the direction of reform by returning the Church to its old position of dominance. They attacked particularly the list of proposed commissioners. In one of the best addresses made during the debate in the Commons, Lyon Playfair, member for the Scottish universities, after chiding the Liberals on their opposition to reform and quoting Pattison on the class character of the two universities, protested that reform could hardly be anticipated from men who were in every instance trained under the system they were asked to reform. He recommended giving to the commission personnel a more imperial complexion as had been done for the Commission for the Scottish Universities.[46]

Grant Duff did not oppose the bill but inquired dramatically, "Why should Oxford strike her flag to Berlin or Heidelberg?" Holding up Appleton's volume, he quoted from it at length. Sayce and Max Müller were both quoted on the need for Oriental languages. "The non-existence at Oxford of any adequate representation of the various branches of knowledge which are especially Indian, is," he declared, "surely one of the very strangest phenomena observable in Europe." After again quoting Pattison, he cited Appleton and Edward Frankland on the achievements of the German universities and the lagging state of Cambridge and Oxford. He urged that the commission's membership be revised to include men familiar with science and with the German universities. "At the beginning of the last century the German Universities were far inferior to our own. A little more than a hundred years later they were far in advance of them; but there is nothing to prevent their respective positions being entirely reversed before the year 1900, if we are only wise now . . ."[47]

The next year an act creating a commission for each of the two universities passed, and the second reform of the two universities was begun.[48] In drawing up the reforms the Commissions were to consult with the Colleges but, except for appeals to the Privy Council, final power lay with them.

Being charged with reform, the Commissions gave short shrift to those who argued against any change or challenged them with unpleasantly searching questions. One thing emerges very clearly from the evidence taken by the Oxford Commission: German universities, German research, and German practices generally constituted the touchstone about which discussion tended to center. One of the Commissioners himself produced the calendars of offerings at the University of Berlin and of Strasbourg University.[49] Two witnesses, J. Cook Wilson and L. R. Phelps, were summoned specifically because they had recently studied in German universities.[50] Next to the German, the Scottish universities were most frequently mentioned. American universities were referred to by Goldwin Smith, who had taught at Cornell and regretted the absence there of the collegiate system. France was mentioned twice, once in connection with anthropology and once in connection with Oriental languages, in both of which she was believed to have retained her old leadership. Other than that, except for an occasional mention of Swiss or Dutch universities, all references were to Germany. Of some seventy-odd witnesses appearing, no less than thirty-three referred to the German universities, their methods or achievements.[51]

Equally significant was the consistency of the reformers' admiration of the Germans and the distaste for German practices expressed by the defenders of the status quo.[52] But the conservatives were at last breaking ranks. Pusey now found it expedient in the interest of defending theological studies to draw attention to the much more extensive provision for that subject in the German universities,[53] and others were admitting that all theological students had now some knowledge of German work.[54] They were, however, far from prepared to agree with the reformers upon "the desirability of founding chairs in the theological faculty without its being necessary for the holders to have any doctrinal test or subscription.[55] And even professionals such as Acland and Maine refused to join in the demand made by E. Ray Lankester and James Bryce for professional schools of medicine and law.[56]

The principal problem confronting the Commissions was to break the teaching monopoly of the colleges and to compel them to use their large endowments in support of professorships and university purposes generally. Actually, the old collegiate tutorial system of instruction was in some measure already breaking down from its inadequacy to meet the changing conditions. Two indications which gave evidence of this were the monopoly by the University of the teaching of science, and the growth of intercollegiate teaching. Except for two or three colleges in each university, the colleges offered no science teaching and admitted that it was impossible, because of the expensive equipment required, to compete with the university save at the most elementary level. The intercollegiate system of teaching, greatly extolled by a number of tutors and the defenders of the existing system, was, the reformers believed, an admission that no college could any longer provide all the instruction necessary for a degree. At the same time, the system failed to provide an orderly pattern of instruction and the teaching remained in the hands of men only superficially qualified.[57]

Since in the two universities the humanistic disciplines had not been recognized as professions, and the tutors had been clerics awaiting college livings, one problem facing the reformers was to make the salaries of the tutors attractive enough to keep them until academic promotion was possible.[58] Another was to make the salaries of the legal and medical faculties attractive enough so that men accepting appointments here would devote their full time to their university duties.[59] Until this time law professors particularly had usually been non-residents and the medical professors had engaged in private practice because few such men either would or could afford to depend exclusively upon the salaries offered them as professors. The solution, as the reformers saw, was a graded system through which the better scholars might advance: tutor, lecturer, reader, professor.[60] But since there were relatively few professorships and very few readerships, more such positions would have to be created and the salaries of all the offices raised.

The demand for research endowment, so prominent in the agitation of the period, while playing an important part in stimulating reform by pointing out the great work being done in Germany, was in part illusory. Several witnesses agreed with Thorold Rogers' statement: "There have been a great many persons of comparative leisure at Oxford for many centuries, and I am not aware that the result has been anything like research."[61] The truth is that research was as foreign a notion in the English universities as was seminar teaching and laboratory teaching. Not that something corresponding to these had never been done, but the average professor or tutor had no conception of what the new men really meant by the terms and little or no sense of any duty to perform whatever might be meant by them. At best they conceived it their duty to "keep up" in their subject. Pusey, Regius Professor of Hebrew, receiving £1500 a year, was a conscientious man who doubtless delivered all of the fifty-four "catechetical" lectures a year which he reported in addition to his canonical duties to Christ Church.[62] But Henry Acland, both Regius Professor of Medicine and professor of clinical medicine, in the first capacity delivered no lectures, merely supervising examinations, and in the latter, only "occasionally" lectured.[63] For this he received in 1876 £639, a modest enough stipend, but his duties left him so much time, had he wanted to do research, that the Commissioners were genuinely puzzled as to how he spent it.[64] Hence what the new men who had acquired "the scientific spirit" had to do was less to reform the institution than to replace the older men with scholars who, like themselves, had been initiated into the joys of scientific research. What was really lacking was not the opportunity but the new conception of university instruction as the search for, rather than the transmission of, knowledge. Only a minority of the professors or tutors had any interest in research and as academic administrators either in the colleges or universities they gave no official recognition to research. As Mark Pattison, whose testimony before this Commission was surprisingly truculent and half-hearted, seems to have realized, in the last analysis "the scientific spirit" could not be legislated into existence nor even, perhaps, greatly affected by institutional change.[65] At most, such changes might encourage it, and this was undoubtedly one of the values, however hard to measure, achieved by the reforms. Beyond that, the development of interest in the prosecution of knowledge was largely the result of the German influence working through the various disciplines.

Faced with these multifarious problems, the Commissions recognized that collegiate teaching was too firmly established to be dislodged and, as many of the most fervent admirers of the German universities, including Max Müller among others, also recognized, the colleges offered special values quite absent from the German scene.[66] These values the Commissioners sought to retain while providing for better teaching in more subjects and a graded professoriate. Since no one was quite sure what the relationship between collegiate and professorial teaching should be, however, the problem was left to internal adjustment, a not unusual means of postponing a solution.

Much attention has been given to the first Parliamentary reform of the universities because it established a precedent; the result has been that the reforms effected by the Statutes of 1882 have been overshadowed. These were at least of equal, perhaps of greater, importance. As the first reform altered collegiate practices, the second changed university practices as a whole. Both contributed to improving the instruction and the intellectual atmosphere. But where the earlier reform got rid of many anachronistic regulations and practices enabling the colleges to operate more efficiently, the latter remodelled the universities in such a way as to give them some claim as universities and not merely as a collection of undergraduate schools.

To illustrate the remarkable changes brought about, one has only to compare the lists of professors, readers, and university lecturers in 1876 with those of 1886.[67] At Oxford in 1876 there were 40 professors and readers, 30 of whom had been appointed before 1870; in the later year there were 63, only 17 of whom had been appointed before 1870, 13 during the 1870's and no less than 34 (over half) who had been appointed since 1880. The figures for Cambridge in 1886 are even more impressive. Of 73 professors, readers, and university lecturers, only 12 had received appointments before 1870, 14 had been appointed in the seventies, and no less than 47 between 1880 and 1886. Of the 39 professors, less than a third had been appointed before 1870, while 14 had been appointed in the eighties, 10 in the two years of 1883 and 1884 alone. This suggests, in addition to the considerable increase in the number of university teachers, the large infusion of new and younger scholars which occurred. It may be doubted that such a revolution in the teaching staff of the two institutions had ever taken place within so short a space of time.

In summary, by the new statutes at both universities, clerical restrictions on the heads of colleges were all but swept away, and clerical fellowships and tutorships were reduced to a minimum. Fellowships, instead of being held for life on condition of celibacy, were freed from that restriction, but made terminal in seven years with renewal possible for those engaged in tuition or other service for college or university. A proportion of the college revenues was to be paid annually to the universities for the maintenance of the new university instructors and such institutions as the university libraries, laboratories, and museums.[68]

Without further detailing the reforms, it may be said that Jowett's ideals were more fully realized than were Pattison's. If reform was inevitable, all but the bitter-enders among the residents could accept the less radical of Jowett's proposals. Professional study was provided more fully in the sciences than in the humanities, where the position of the professors remained anomalous. Fellowships were more frequently awarded for research purposes, and the doctoral degree, in the few instances where it was awarded, increasingly implied distinction proven by academic achievement. But a collegiate education remained the ideal norm though specialization entered even there, after responsions or the previous examinations were passed.

If Pattison's ideals received little institutional recognition, they were far from lost. Writing in 1885, the distinguished Russian historian, Paul Vinogradoff, found the work of the English universities in philology and history in a state of "comparative barrenness" compared to the German. What was badly needed was the "practical work" of the seminar, an innovation which was to await his own coming to Oxford in history in 1904. Meanwhile he believed that nothing better could be said of the needs of Oxford than what Mark Pattison had already written.[69] And Pattison's ideas continued to form the basis for agitation and slow change by small reforms within the universities until after World War I when Parliament again intervened.[70]

The situation in the two ancient universities in the seventies and eighties was deprecatingly but accurately described by H. A. L. Fisher:

> While Oxford and Cambridge once liberated from the thraldom of religious tests reverberated with the echoes of Teutonic learning, the more eminent professors of Berlin or Goettingen could count upon a band of young English admirers, who, returning to their more civilised but less erudite compatriots, preached the majesty of German knowledge.[71]

But whatever the follies and fanaticisms of the English scholars and scientists who came under the German influence, it must be acknowledged that it was they who, as leaders among the tutors, lecturers, and professors during the third quarter of the century, were remolding university instruction into more effective form.

Accepting the importance of systematic, specialized study both for students and teachers, and thinking increasingly in national and secular, rather than insular and Anglican, terms, they sought to strengthen teaching and scholarship by professionalizing them and extending the curriculum to include a wide variety of subjects. Having adopted the conception of the scholar-teacher devoted to his special subject, further reform became inevitable and the old conception of a collegiate education, predominantly undergraduate, character-training and mind-forming, gave way, for the more scholarly, to the conception of a university education designed to provide professional competence in some special study as the ultimate ideal. Seeking to reform the two universities from within, these scholars and scientists joined in the demands for reform from without in the seventies and met with some success in bringing Cambridge and Oxford into the mainstream of the intellectual development of the West without wholly sacrificing the original ideals of a liberal education. The modern reputation of the two universities dates from this reform.

The English, however, remained sceptical of a paternalism, a professionalism, and an efficiency dependent in any way upon the state and left all education above the elementary level almost wholly dependent upon voluntary effort on the part of individuals and their families. There were aids in the form of scholarships administered by the individual colleges but little encouragement otherwise. No easy channels were provided for any but the wealthy to pass from the elementary school to higher learning, and all commentators agree that during the years after the second Parliamentary reform fewer poor men found their way to Oxford or Cambridge than at almost any time in their long histories.[72] They remained class institutions, despite the extension courses and summer schools for adults, but what had originally been a religious class distinction became increasingly a financial class distinction.

The pressures of a rapidly expanding scientific, industrial, national society, expertly utilized by the Germans, compelled the English to move in a direction where their own traditions, impeding progress, may be said to have failed them, as the Germans were aided by theirs. In borrowing from the Germans, the English modified and adapted in their inimitable fashion until the measures taken assumed the very color and temper of their own institutional traditions, so minimizing the reforms by blunting their effectiveness in the interest of retaining certain cherished values of their own.

3.

Hegelianism, imperialism, and state socialism

The "nationalization" of the two ancient universities, though only a beginning was made by the eighties, was part of a larger movement: the secularization of thought and the substitution of the State for the Church as the institutional focus of man's purpose in the world. Before the Parliamentary reforms of the fifties, Oxford and Cambridge were little more than inefficient schools for a particular religious group who also played a large part in controlling the state. After the reforms of 1882 they were in a sense state-supervised, though not state-supported, institutions to prepare men for the professions and the service of the state.

Secularism was, however, only one aspect of the thought of the period and perhaps, as Mark Pattison suggested, not the predominant trend in the universities after 1870. Though the German idealist movement had sympathies with religious thought and faith, belief in a metaphysical system is not precisely equivalent to religious belief. A metaphysical system, as a logical exposition of a conception of the world, may approximate or even support a religious belief. It does not, however, necessarily do so; it frequently replaces it. And the tendency in this period to replace religious creeds and faiths with metaphysical beliefs suggests that what may be distinguished as ideologies were beginning to replace religions, a movement probably associated with professionalism.

Testifying before the Select Committee on University Tests in 1871, the Hegelian, C. A. Appleton, reported that "the ideas which are now prevalent at Oxford . . . are for the most part the ideas of thinkers in Germany."[73] Their effect was to make it "quite impossible for any man to throw himself into the system of education for the final classical school at Oxford . . . without having the whole edifice of belief shaken to the very foundation. At the same time the agencies which are brought to bear upon him, the philosophical ideas and modes of criticism, not only destroy but ultimately reconstruct belief . . ."[74] But this reconstruction of belief was not a return to the old faith without serious alteration. It was, as Appleton's life and work testified, a belief in professional study, in secular institutions, and notably in the State as representative of the Absolute.

The Anglican Church did not, of course, cease to be an important force in English life, but its influence was reduced and such power as it retained was exercised increasingly as an independent auxiliary rather than as a twin power with the state. Its rank became that of a junior partner, a rank which in all but certain official circumstances it shared with an ever-growing number of other institutions. The elevation of the state or the secular community into a predominant position was an ironic result of the Broad Churchmen's emphasis upon the national functions of the Church.

As the English Churchmen had been helped to their conclusions by German ideas, so the process of exalting the state among the empiricists and positivists was greatly aided by German thought and practice. The intellectual history of Germany in the nineteenth century may, with necessary exceptions, be summarily described as a continuous movement away from idealist metaphysics towards either positivism or dialectical materialism. The work of the German scholars had originated in an effort to elaborate and complete the insights of the great metaphysicians and, with that end in view, to create a *Kulturgeschichte* which would ideally reveal in concrete detail the abstruse conceptions of a dynamically evolving *Geist*. But in pursuit of this aim, they were led by the desire to furnish unquestionable proof of their contentions to adopting the methods of the Enlightenment, the philological methods of Bentley and Porson, the methods of biblical and historical criticism, and the methods of the Newtonian sciences. The result was that, becoming specialists and technologists, they departed ever farther from their original intention until any resemblance to it became almost accidental.

M. E. Sadler, who had himself studied in German universities, wrote in the nineties that:

... concerted specialisation of the German type is only possible when the scattered parts, which form the whole, are held together by some large controlling power, recognised and obeyed by every single agent in the great undertaking ... In the highest types of concerted intellectual effort, this place of dominant authority is not occupied by the administrative Government. In the greatest and most fruitful intellectual movements, the really dominant authority has always been not administrative in character, but intellectual or (in the largest sense of the word) spiritual. The binding idea which most firmly holds together the intellectual labours of men engaged in the building up of knowledge is the conception of the unity of all knowledge and the conviction that all individual research and labour should be subordinated to the claims of knowledge as a whole and of society as a whole. This idea may seem dim and shadowy and transcendental, but nevertheless it has always been a very real and potent force in the minds of those who have done the most illustrious deeds in the field of scientific research.[75]

Sadler was himself a philosophical idealist and he recognized at the time this was written, that the "binding idea," if it existed in Germany, had been greatly altered from the early nineteenth century. It was by the seventies less a conception of the unity of knowledge than of society as a whole, or the national state, to which intellectual labors were being subordinated. As early as the fifties and sixties a conception of knowledge as a spiritual unity had seemed, indeed, not merely transcendental, (a German could do with that) but extremely "dim and shadowy." The metaphysical systems which had originally provided the unifying element declined in influence as the historical and scientific methodology gained acceptance.

An indication of this appeared not only in the Hegelianism of the left, culminating in the work of Karl Marx, but also in the revival of an agnostic Kantianism in philosophic thought and in the dropping of the "encyclopedic" courses from the curriculum in the German universities as philosophy itself divided into a host of specialties.[76] Instead of the all-embracing courses appeared those massive encyclopedias of collected monographs, the graveyards of nineteenth century learning.[77]

As the lines of connection between the varied specialized studies became ever more tenuous, such unity as they appeared to have was due primarily to the fact that they were historical. The special studies were no longer conceived as subordinate parts within overarching metaphysical systems of belief but as branches of study having a common methodology. Induction rather than deduction would furnish the key to all the mysteries, and unity of knowledge came to be regarded as an end to be attained, rather than as something logically pre-existing. When the binding idea was not simply conceived as service to the national state, it was thought of as some kind of unified structure, something on the order of the great Indo-European tree of languages, organically connected, which would, as had that, become visible when finally all the varied parts were sufficiently elaborated.

So far from their original sources of inspiration had the majority of German scholars departed by the sixties and seventies that it was possible to see their scholarly work in isolation, as it were, from its metaphysical foundations. The original whole had fallen away, leaving only its outlying parts, each sporting its independence. Young Englishmen like Ingram Bywater, trained in Mill and Comte under Mark Pattison's tutelage, appeared never to have suspected the original import that the study of Greek philology had for his German masters. The positivist scholar could thus ignore the metaphysical implications of the German work since many, if not most, German scholars were ignoring it themselves. Understanding this, we can better understand how it was that positivism as a practicing faith, as distinct from positivism as theoretical dogma, entered English scholarship and science from German at least as much as from French sources. We can also understand the simultaneous appearance in the most diverse subjects of the German influence in Britain, even when the men influenced, like Tylor, remained unreconstructed empiricists.

Although the influence of German thought appeared in its most concentrated form in the old universities during these years, it was to be encountered as well among many leaders of thought in

England outside the universities. The great Unitarian leader, James Martineau, had received what he called a "second education" at the University of Berlin.[78] His student, Richard Holt Hutton, friend of Bagehot at University College, London, studied at Heidelberg, Berlin, and Bonn, and assisted Bagehot as editor of the *Economist* before becoming editor and later co-proprietor of the *Spectator* for thirty-five years.[79] When in the seventies George Grote founded *Mind*, a journal of philosophy with an empirical, positivist policy, he chose as its editor the Scotsman, George Croom Robertson, assistant to Bain at Aberdeen who, after study at University College, London, had gone to Heidelberg, Berlin, and Göttingen, as well as to Paris.[80]

If, as has frequently been observed, the climate of opinion in Germany and England in the eighties exhibited many similarities, that was because the two countries had deeply influenced each other. Both Germany and England were becoming what, for lack of a better word, we must call Europeanized. What seemed to unite the work of the scholars and scientists of both countries, as well as of other countries in Western European society, was by that date usually phrased as "the pursuit of knowledge" or the "discovery of truth." But except among the idealists, such knowledge or truth was by definition not metaphysical. The very fervor of this faith in the value of knowledge or truth often seemed to hint at divinity, and for many, doubtless, it meant something between the deistic conception of natural law as divine ordinance and the more mystical conceptions of the pantheist. Yet that this truth pertained solely to the social or historical universe they would only reluctantly have denied.

Among many positivists, if under that term we may include convinced anti-metaphysical minds of all descriptions, and particularly among the artists, scholars, and scientists of that persuasion, specialization was carried to its extreme conclusion. Indifferent to the social or political relevance of their discoveries, and pushing to its logical conclusion the search for truth or knowledge, they became devotees of "pure" research or of "pure" art. The emergence of a doctrine of art for art's sake paralleled the emergence of the doctrines of scholarship for scholarship's sake, of science for science's sake, of knowledge for the sake of knowledge. While an extreme conclusion at once of individualism and specialization, this position in a purely secular, naturalistic world may, in the light of its devotees' consecration to their professional disciplines, be regarded as analagous to the position of the monk or mystic in a religiously oriented world. Like their contemporaries among the religious believers who clung to a faith without creed or ritual, many artists, scholars, and scientists zealously devoted their lives to the service of an unchurched and unknown god.

Apart from these purists, the positivists turned to the state for recognition of their professions, to spread their learning, to adopt their findings to its needs, and to promote their own researches. To strengthen the state by organizing more efficiently its subsidiary institutions was an impelling motive behind the efforts of many scientists, scholars, and technologists. This interest in institutionalizing under the auspices of the central government brought them into common contention with the philosophical idealists.

Dismayed by the growing intellectual anarchy, philosophic idealism attracted those speculative minds in England who were seeking a unified meaning of the world; but Hegelian idealism provided not only metaphysical solace but a view of the national state as a systematically, organically related spiritual whole. The idealists were less concerned than the positivists with the practical problems involved in strengthening the state's power, though some, and particularly their students, did their part in that respect also, rather than asserting the state's spiritual and moral character and its intrinsic and substantial reality within the passing flux. However, with one group providing a spiritual and moral impulse and the other furnishing practical proposals, each in its own way supported institutionalizing, professionalizing, and nationalizing their society. And as the interests of eternity gave way to contemporary social interests and these two groups each in their own way supported the national state, the history of the national state became the principal synthetic subject.

In the study of history with its emphasis upon the rise of the national state, the comparative method inevitably brought England into immediate comparison with other states, and particularly with Germany and the United States. The Teutonic or Aryan conception of the philological, cultural, and racial homogeneity of these three nations served as a golden cord to bind them together. Among the more sanguine and speculative, this encouraged the vision of a Teutonic or Saxon world order, a vision which endured long after these decades. Among the less sanguine and more realistic, the comparison, strongly influenced also by contemporary events, served to bring Britain into an increasingly unpleasant, however informative, juxtaposition.

The great contrast found between Britain and Germany turned invariably on the disorganized institutional situation in the former and the highly organized institutional situation in the latter. This theme was developed in every subject and every activity during the decades after 1866 and in every case the example of Germany was cited to urge extension of state activity in the interest of more efficient order. At home, such activity was not only in the interest of institutional reform but also of social reconstruction; abroad, it was in the interest of imperial power.

The movements of socialism and imperialism were alike being prepared for in the universities of the seventies and eighties. At the moment when Matthew Arnold wrote sentimentally of Oxford as the home of lost causes, it was becoming the champion of new ones. The Canadian, George Parkin, who attended Oxford in the early seventies and became a tireless advocate of imperial federation, declared later that "the influences then at work to mould thought or character in the University were what I can only describe as dynamic." Among the influences he specified were those of Ruskin, Dean Stanley, who occasionally delivered sermons, T. H. Green, Max Müller, "and Bonamy Price, once Arnold's right hand man at Rugby."[81] Parkin was fortunate to find himself at Balliol, the active center of the new influences, and a college which during Jowett's administration produced three successive viceroys of India: Lansdowne (1888–1893), Elgin (1894–1899), and Curzon (1899–1904). Any time in the seventies or eighties Parkin would have encountered sympathetic minds there. In addition to Edward Grey, Henry Asquith, Alfred Milner, Balliol contributed many other men to the service of the state in one way or another. Among others were Clinton Dawkins, James Rennell Rodd, Cecil Spring-Rice, Arthur Hardinge, Louis Mallet, Bernard Mallet, George Leveson-Gower, Anthony Hope Hawkins; among journalists with political influence were Leopold Amery, J. St. Loe Strachey, E. T. Cooke, Sidney Lowe, and J. A. Spender.[82] With few exceptions these men were imperialists, Liberal or Conservative, and were among the most influential men in Great Britain in the two decades before 1914. Other colleges also contributed their share of imperialists and all contributed workers to the cause of alleviating the condition of the lower classes through education and mission work or through reform activities.

Imperialism and social reconstruction were in their origins twin movements and the association of Imperialism and Tory Democracy made by Disraeli was no yoking of incompatibles. In his inaugural address at Oxford in 1870 Ruskin, the social reformer, denouncing materialism and mammon-worship in words echoing Carlyle, urged Colonial expansion upon England: "This is what she must do, or perish: she must found colonies as fast and as far as she is able . . . seizing every piece of fruitful waste ground she can set her foot on, and there teaching these her colonists that their first aim is to be to advance the power of England by land and sea . . ."[83] The urgency of this sprang probably from the contemporary events on the Continent, events which were to frighten more stable characters than Ruskin. At the same time he was busy, as on his famous road near Oxford, persuading undergraduates such as Cecil Rhodes and Alfred Milner to work for the good of society.

As service to the Church declined in favor, service to society or the state became the conscious goal of the more serious men in the universities, whether the impulse came from Carlyle, Ruskin, Jowett, T. H. Green, F. H. Bradley, Bernard Bosanquet, Arnold Toynbee, Seeley, William Cunningham, or others. Social reform and imperialism were the dynamic new movements in the years following 1866, years during which the men who were to guide British destinies in the dreadful second decade of the twentieth century were being educated. Not only did these movements profit by the substitution of the state for the church as the focus of men's thought and the growing concern for greater institutional order, both of which owed so much to the German idealist influence; but they owed nearly as much to the frightened response of the English to the appearance of the new German Empire, which from the very moment of its origin, threatened by virtue of its military might to become the predominant power on the Continent, and perhaps in the world.

Notes

CHAPTER IV

1. See Montagu Burrows, "Inaugural Lecture," privately printed (Oxford, 1862).

2. See William Austen Leigh in *Augustus Austen Leigh* (London, 1906), pp. 84–86, 138–140 for a discussion of the problem as it arose at King's College, Cambridge.

3. Benjamin Jowett, "Suggestions for University Reform, 1874" in Lewis Campbell, *The Nationalization of the Old Universities* (London, 1901), pp. 183 ff.

4. "Partly the restriction of celibacy, and partly the very smallness of the salaries . . . have commonly prevented college tuition from being regarded as a regular profession." Henry Sidgwick in "Idle Fellowships," *Contemporary Review*, 27 (1875–1876), p. 683. Cf., George Charles Broderick, *Memories and Impressions* (London, 1900), p. 344.

5. Leigh, *op. cit.*, 139.

6. This has been admirably set forth by Eric Ashby, *Technology and the Academics* (London, 1959), in a chapter entitled "Split Personality in Universities." See esp. p. 88. Also Report of the Rev. M. Pattison, *P. P.* 1861 [2794–IV].

7. Quoted by Roll-Hansen, p. 86 from Pattison's obituary notice in the *Academy*, XIX (1881), p. 127. See Roll-Hansen's discussion, pp. 75 ff. on the differences between Pattison and Jowett.

8. See in Coons, *op. cit.* (note 35, Chapter II above), p. 45, the account of an "unofficial association of younger dons which met two or three times a term in 1876 and 1877 and formulated a liberal programme."

9. Quoted by Tillyard, *op. cit.* (note 25, Chapter II above), pp. 187–188. Cf., V. H. H. Green, *Oxford Common Room: A Study of Lincoln College and Mark Pattison* (London, 1957), Ch. XI.

10. Mark Pattison, *Suggestions on Academical Organization, with Especial Reference to Oxford* (London, 1868), pp. 157–167.

11. Select Committee on the Oxford and Cambridge Universities

Education Bill, 1867 (497), XIII, 2419. This will be referred to here-after as "Education Bill"; See also for Jowett's position, First Report from the Select Committee of the House of Lords on University Tests; with Minutes of Evidence Appended, Session 1871 (179 Report), (17, Minutes of Evidence) London, 1871. Referred to hereafter as "University Tests"; Report of the University of Oxford Commission, 1881 [C. 2868], LVI, referred to hereafter as "Oxford Commission"; and Jowett's "Suggestions for University Reform, 1874," apparently given in full in Lewis Campbell, *op. cit.*, pp. 183–208.

12. J. A. Froude in his "Inaugural Address at the University of St. Andrew's," *Short Studies*, p. 319, observed that the subject was "on everybody's lips."

13. See Hansard, 3rd Series, 187 (1867), 1613–1614.

14. *Ibid.*, 1615.

15. Geoffrey Faber, *Jowett* (Cambridge, 1957) pp. 348–350; and Hansard, *op cit.*, 1632–1634.

16. Hansard, *op. cit.*, 1636–1641.

17. Hansard, 3rd Series, 158 (1857), 1217–1218.

18. Hansard, 3rd Series, 187 (1867), 1619–1623.

19. Education Bill, 2566.

20. Education Bill, 2566.

21. William Walrond Jackson, *Ingram Bywater, 1840–1914* (Oxford, 1917); and "Duff, Mountstuart Elphinstone Grant," *D. N. B.*

22. Education Bill, 1470, 1472.

23. Education Bill, 2424–26.

24. Education Bill, 3252–3361.

25. Education Bill, 3301–3316.

26. Education Bill, 4207–4485.

27. James M. Hart, *German Universities* (New York, 1874), p. 334.

28. Charles Astor Bristed, *Five Years in an English University* (New York, 1874). Originally written in 1851, this was a revised edition, but it is not, of course, strictly comparable to Hart's account.

29. Bristed, p. 394, attributed the English scholars' reluctance to publish to "false modesty and an excessive fastidiousness produced by hypercriticism."

30. Mrs. Creighton, *op. cit.*, (note 35, Chapter II above), I, p. 333.

31. "Oxford and Cambridge are not part of the republic of letters but a privileged literary order." So wrote Samuel Gray Ward in a letter to Charles Eliot Norton, c. 1866, Ward Papers, Harvard University Library.

32. *Saturday Review*, 2 March 1867, quoted by Hutton, p. 119.

33. See John H. Appleton and A. H. Sayce, *Dr. Appleton: His Life and Literary Relics* (London, 1881), p. 16.

34. See Roll-Hansen, *op. cit.* (note I, Chapter II above), pp. 82, and 108 ff.

35. See Ch. III, above, notes No. 35, 36.

36. Roll-Hansen, *op. cit.*, p. 67.

37. *Ibid.*, pp. 81–82.

38. For example T. K. Cheyne, in *Essays on the Endowment of Research by Various Writers* (London, 1876), p. 188, wrote: "Travelling scholarships should be founded for young men of small means to complete their studies at a German university;" and Henry Nettleship, pp. 258–259, wrote: "If a man wishes to make himself a thorough scholar, he must go to Germany and learn method there."

39. See Ch. III, note No. 21.

40. See "Report of the Syndicate Appointed May 27, 1875 to Consider Requirements of the University in Different Departments of Study," *Cambridge University Reporter*, No. 148 (March 17, 1876), pp. 297–358; and "Statement of the Requirements of the University adopted by the Hebdomadal Council on the 19th of March, 1877." *Supplement* to *Oxford University Gazette*, No. 254 (April 28, 1877).

41. V. H. H. Green, p. 250; Winstanley, *Later Victorian Cambridge* (Cambridge, 1947), pp. 271–272.

42. As early as the hearings on the question of religious tests, Lord Salisbury seems to have felt that university reform was probably inevitable; see University Tests, 116. In the Commons, Beresford Hope, not a reformer as we have seen, supported the Conservative motion, urging that the bill be hurried through (Hansard, 3rd Series, CCXXX [1876], 1085 ff.). Sir John Mowbray, another Conservative, accused the Liberals of "wanting to defeat the bill in order that the glory of the reform would be the Liberal Party's." *Ibid.*, 1120.

43. Hansard, 3rd Series, CCXXVII (1876), 791–802.

44. *Ibid.*, 803–804.

45. Hansard, 3rd Series, CCXXVIII (1876), 263.

46. Hansard, 3rd Series, CCXXX (1876), 1068–1078.

47. *Ibid.*, 1098–1110.

48. Tillyard, *op. cit.* (note 32, Chapter III above), pp. 211–219.

49. Oxford Commission, 1881.

50. *Ibid.*, 866, 919.

51. My calculation.

52. See in Oxford Commission, H. W. Chandler's testimony, 1663 ff. and J. R. Magrath, 2224 ff., esp. 2316–2318. Cf., Winstanley, *op. cit.* (note 34, Chapter III above), p. 269.

53. *Ibid.*, 4578 ff.

54. *Ibid.*, 4537.

55. *Ibid.*, 4659.

56. *Ibid.*, Bryce, 1420–1439; Maine, 5627; Acland, 3107; Lankester, 5203.

57. *Ibid.*, G. G. Bradley, 2086; A. Robinson, 2563; W. W. Capes, 3882 ff.

58. As early as December, 1872, Trinity College, Cambridge, attempted to revise its statutes partly to meet this situation. But since

the Parliament was preparing to reform the University as a whole, the Privy Council refused to sanction new statutes for a single college. Among the more active reformers in that College were Coutts Trotter (University of Berlin), Henry Sidgwick (University of Dresden), Robert Burn, Henry Jackson, R. C. Jebb, and the Master of the College, W. H. Thompson. See Winstanley, *op. cit.* (note 34, Chapter III above), Ch. VI.

59. Particularly the law professors at both universities were non-residents until the eighties because few sufficiently eminent men would or could afford to depend upon the salaries offered them as professors. See Oxford Commission, 1018–1032, 1059–1063, 1207–1210; and Sidgwick, *op. cit.* (note 32, Chapter III above), p. 680.

60. Thomas Fowler, who had already written on this subject in an article, "On Examinations," *Fortnightly*, N.S. XIX (1876), 418–429, and Jowett both pointed this out to the Oxford Commission, 1563–1568, and 2664–2669.

61. Oxford Commission, 2876. This was the position of the Utilitarians generally.

62. "Return of Certain Particulars with regard to the Universities of Oxford and Cambridge," House of Commons, 1876 (349), p. 12. Hereafter this is referred to as Certain Particulars, 1876.

63. Oxford Commission, 3128–3148, and Certain Particulars, 1876, p. 12.

64. Part of Acland's testimony is too revealing to ignore. "I should like to put it on record that great pains have been taken for several years to render that institution [the Infirmary] available as an example of a well-arranged sanitary hospital, and generally *to prepare it for anything which your Commission or any other authority should suggest* to be desirable. We have built there a clinical laboratory so that *work could be begun if you desire it.* Oxford Commission, 3107 (my emphasis).

65. See his opening statement (Oxford Commission, 4115) in which he said in part: "It will be said . . . that it is an evil which your Commission could not reach. I feel the force of this objection. To come before you with this complaint is to ask you to lay your hands on our heads and convey to us a new spirit, the spirit of the pursuit of science and learning." Cf., Green, pp. 251 ff.

66. Oxford Commission, 3427. The majority were naturally strongly attached to the collegiate system.

67. Certain Particulars, 1876, and Return of Certain Particulars with regard to the Universities of Oxford and Cambridge, House of Commons, 1886 (214). The following figures are all derived from these two sources; the calculations are mine.

68. For fuller accounts see Tillyard, *op. cit.* (note 32, Chapter III above), pp. 219–232; for Cambridge the story is told at length by Winstanley, *op. cit.* (note 34, Chapter III above), Ch. VII; C. E.

Mallet, *A History of the University of Oxford* (New York, 1928), III, pp. 340–353, is brief for Oxford. See also G. W. Hemming, "The Past and Future of Cambridge University," *Nineteenth Century*, 13 (1883), pp. 824–840.

69. Paul Vinogradoff, "Oxford and Cambridge through Foreign Spectacles," *Fortnightly Review*, 43 (1885), pp. 866–867 esp.

70. See Report, Royal Commission on Oxford and Cambridge Universities, 1922 [C. 1588], pp. 25 ff. The arguments will be found to resemble remarkably those of the nineteenth century. See also Farnell, *op. cit.*, (note 28, Chapter VII, above), pp. 105 ff., F. Haverfield, ed. *Essays* by Henry Francis Pelham (Oxford, 1911), pp. vii–xxiii; Oona Howard Bell, *Sidney Ball* (Oxford, 1923), esp. 189–201.

71. Quoted from his *History of Europe* by Hermann Levy, *England and Germany* (London, 1949), p. 9.

72. Mallet, III, p. 352. Both Lord Curzon *Principles and Methods of University Reform* (Oxford, 1909), Ch. III, and Tillyard *op. cit.* (note 32, Chapter III above), (pp. 354–362) addressed themselves to the problem.

73. See University Tests, Minutes of Evidence, 491.

74. University Tests, 490.

75. M. E. Sadler, "The Unrest in Secondary Education in Germany and Elsewhere," in Gt. Britain, Board of Education, Special Reports on Educational Subjects, [Cd. 836], vol. 9, Education in Germany, London, 1902, p. 35.

76. See Merz, *op. cit.* (note 3, Chapter I above), I, pp. 34–36.

77. *Ibid.*, I, p. 35, the footnote esp.

78. Meyrick H. Carré, *Phases of Thought in England* (Oxford, 1949), p. 362.

79. "Hutton, Richard Holt," *D. N. B.*

80. See "Robertson, George Croom," *D. N. B.*

81. Sir John Willison, *Sir George Parkin* (London, 1929), pp. 28–29. See Herbert Henry Asquith, *Memories and Reflections, 1852–1927* (Boston, 1928), pp. 22–48.

82. See Sir James Rennell Rodd, *Social and Diplomatic Memories, 1884–1893* (London, 1922), p. 7, and J. A. Spender, *Life, Journalism and Politics* (London, 1927), I, p. 18, note.

83. Quoted by C. A. Bodelsen, *Studies in Mid-Victorian Imperialism* (Christiana, 1924), p. 105, n. 2.

Campaigns for National Efficiency in Education

When in the nineties fear of German industrial competition attained its greatest height, educational and scientific reformers had again become active as on previous similar occasions. The added tensions of failure on the battlefield and administration during the Boer War, and the growing fear of Germany generated new campaigns to improve education at every level. The revelations of educational deficiency by the war commissions, the consular reports of the decline in Britain's ability to compete commercially, and new accounts of Germany's educational provisions, focused attention upon England's backwardness. Slowly the importance of formal education for industry, commerce, agriculture, engineering, and medicine, as well as for the army and navy, was becoming more widely recognized. But the new converts to the cause of formal education were not being won by the old ideals of liberal education nor by the older institutions of learning.

Arthur Balfour, student of the German-inspired idealists and himself an idealist philosopher as well as a statesman, understood what English education had neglected. To students at Manchester he pointed out that they had "something more than personal responsibility, something more than the desire for self-advancement" to consider. "They were concerned in a national work, and ought to look at it from a national point of view."[1] And in 1899, after outlining the conception of liberal education, he continued: "But there is another side, and, from a national point of view, perhaps a decidedly more important side than that, and the side I mean is the complete scientific equipment of a student for those professions in which a thorough grounding in science, theoretical and practical, is absolutely necessary if he is to make the most of himself and the most of the profession in which he is engaged. I have always been deeply interested in this aspect of the question, which is one specially considered in Germany and elsewhere, and the value of which we have perhaps in this country until recent years unduly ignored and neglected."[2]

Liberal education alone evoked private but little public interest, and as long as education in England had at best a peripheral bearing upon the principal interests of the industrialists and statesmen, they were indifferent about expending large sums of money upon it. In contrast to English indifference and failure to provide funds for formal education, English observers repeatedly pointed to the "German devotion to the claims of knowledge" and the American people's belief in and generous support of education.[3] But behind the devotion to and belief in education in both Germany and the United States lay a close association of formal education with agriculture, industry, professional training, and state service. Since this was less clear in the United States and since in higher education and particularly science education the German model was closely followed, Germany continued to be the primary, though by no means only, example cited by the English reformers, as it was German efficiency they principally feared.

Beginning in the nineties a number of great educational philanthropists appeared in England. These were frequently naturalized German Jews, usually educated in Germany. Included among them were Alfred and Otto Beit and Julius Wernher, South African millionaires; Ernest Cassell and the Rothschilds, financial magnates; Ludwig Mond, trained at the Universities of Marburg and Heidelberg,[4] founder with J. T. Brunner, of the great chemical firm of Brunner, Mond & Co.; and Ivan Levinstein, trained at the University of Berlin and the Technical High School,[5] founder of the largest manufactory of synthetic dyes in England; one at least, was an American, Andrew Carnegie.

With the exception of Alfred Beit's generous foundation of a chair in colonial history at Oxford at L. S. Amery's suggestion,[6] a grant of £200 per annum for ten years made by Julius Wernher for the Taylorian professor of German,[7] and a Rothschild contribution to a Cambridge physics laboratory, these men either refused to contribute to the old universities or ignored them.[8] What they valued was for the most part formal training in science and technology, as suggested by Mond's gift of the Davy-Faraday Laboratory to the Royal Institution and by the founding of the Schorlemmer Laboratory for organic chemistry at Owens College in the mid-nineties.[9] Englishmen, unless they were technologists, like the chemical manufacturer E. K. Muspratt, who had studied with Hoffman at the old College of Chemistry, or the naval engineer, Alfred Yarrow, were more likely to make large donations to medical research or to hospitals. To men trained in other lands, the British were to be heavily indebted for a large proportion of such scientific and advanced educational facilities as they had by 1914.

The donations of the philanthropists were largely responses to the campaigns begun after 1893 and carried on without a break until 1914 by the scientists and scholars, of whom many were German-trained, and by statesmen and businessmen who recognized the threat to industry or the danger to the country generally posed by Germany.

1.

London University reform and founding the civic universities

For two decades schemes for the reform of London University had been under discussion when, in 1892, a Royal Commission was appointed under the chairmanship of Lord Cowper to study the proposed Gresham University for London. London University, governed by a senate elected by Convocation, in practice all graduates who cared to vote, had as its principal functions to set the syllabi for the examinations, secure and pay the examiners, and award the degrees. Since degree-granting was reserved to a very few institutions in England and the right was jealously guarded, the interests involved in any alteration of the constitution of the University with this privilege were legion, including a variety of London colleges and many others throughout the country, the medical schools of the London hospitals, a large number of technical colleges, the Inns of Court, the Royal College of Physicians, the Royal College of Surgeons, and individual holders of the University's degrees. Whenever proposals for change were made, the institutions were torn between fear of being included or excluded, uncertain which would be worse from their particular viewpoint; the graduates, fearing a devaluation of their degrees, supported the status quo. Partly to avoid the opposition of the latter the notion of a second university, an Albert or a Gresham university was proposed. In addition, there was a division between those who thought of the University primarily as a regional London institution and those who thought it should be regarded as an educational institution for the whole Empire.[10]

With a new Commission in view, Karl Pearson formed an Association for Promoting a Professorial University for London in 1893.[11] What Pearson wanted was to found a university in London on the model of the University of Berlin, and he soon had enrolled some 150 members in the new association. Many were men with whose names we have already become familiar, though there were of course new ones also. The vice-presidents of the Association were Henry Rosoce and the Reverend Frank Bright, Master of University College, Oxford. Of the 147 men signing the Association's statement, 66 were fellows of the Royal Society; most of the Oxford reformers' names who were the intellectual heirs of Pattison appeared, and a few who were not teachers in some English college like Ludwig Mond, Thomas Hardy and George Meredith. So was inaugurated a battle fought over much the same issues as in the 1820's but to be waged at the end of the century in more sophisticated terms.

A division soon appeared among the membership. When Pearson said he wanted to establish a university in London on the model of the University of Berlin he meant it, as did many of his associates, without compromise. To accomplish this, as William Ramsay said when asked by the Gresham Commission why he had withdrawn from the Association, would be politically and administratively impossible in London. Other older scientists with administrative experience, such as W. T. Thistleton-Dyer, Michael Foster, and Norman Lockyer, agreed and thought it also undesirable.[12]

Something of this disagreement probably led to the appointment of the aging Huxley as president of the new Association. For immediately Huxley opposed the original plan. The upshot was Pearson's resignation in a public letter to which Huxley replied. Commenting on the dispute, Lockyer wrote:

> Professor Pearson declares that he desires a University on the model of Berlin; but the question at once arises, Is the model to be followed exactly, or are modifications to be introduced? . . . Prof. Huxley desires that it shall be free, and under existing circumstances we cordially agree with him . . . The external element furnished in Germany by State control must in England be supplied by lay members of the Governing Body, and the difference thus established will run throughout the whole of the Constitution.[13]

Huxley not only opposed government control, but also control wholly by the professors, something many in the association ardently wished.[14] Despite these differences in the method of university government, however, the end result desired by all these men was much the same.

At issue in many discussions before the Gresham Commission were two different conceptions of education in particular. One was that of many of the medical men and the more conservative college teachers who conceived of education as the mastery of a syllabus or body of material by the student who should be tested by outside examiners. Against this utilitarian conception were arrayed all those who had been influenced by the German system directly or indirectly: the scientists, including the philologists and physiologists, the technologists, including some of the physicians and engineers.[15] Because the technologists, however, had had to develop schools outside the universities, many were suspicious of becoming associated with any university, fearing control of the examinations would mean outside examiners. But if that could be avoided, as the others of their group insisted that it should be, they united with the scientists in the Association for the Promotion of a Professorial University for London. In their testimony before the Commission, the members of the Association strongly supported a teaching university in which the teachers controlled their own examinations, the students conducted research, and advanced degrees were awarded only for research.[16] Opposition to the Gresham scheme was strong, but the Association had no practical proposals for organizing from existing conditions what they wanted.

The report of the Commission on the whole supported the desire for reform and made clear the driving force behind it.

> Independent institutions are specially required for the study of those branches of scientific research which are either neglected or so inadequately represented in England that advanced students cross the Channel in order to find elsewhere what a teaching University in London certainly ought to provide. We do not wish to dilate on the very large sums of money spent in Germany and other countries in order to keep abreast of the great scientific movements of the present day; but we think it our duty to state that for the condition of things in London—as compared with the facilities given, for instance by so small a state as Zurich—no excuse can be found.[17]

Again a little further on the Report stated:

> It does not seem possible under present conditions to rival the completeness of the great University of Berlin, where—to take the single example of History—there exist, for Ancient History 3 Professors *Ordinarii*, for Medieval and Modern History 3 Professors *Ordinarii* and 3 *Extra-Ordinarii*, besides other Professors and more than 10 *Privat-Dozenten* dealing with historical subjects.[18]

Though the report offered little in the way of constructive suggestions, it excited the interest of two men who were working for "national efficiency" particularly in Education; Haldane, whose cousin, John Burdon-Sanderson, had served on the Commission, and Sidney Webb. Haldane had been a friend of the Webbs since the eighties. These two men now drafted a plan for a teaching University of London, Webb being careful to include his pet project, the London School of Economics and Politics, still struggling for its existence, along with numerous technical, medical, and other schools and the under-graduate colleges.[19] After two attempts to introduce their draft proposals as a private measure in Parliament, Haldane turned to his friend in the Conservative Cabinet, A. J. Balfour, who undertook to have the plan introduced in the Commons by Sir John Gorst of the Education Department. It brought under one institution the two university colleges of London, the principal technical schools, and a variety of other institutions. Strongly supported in the Commons by Bryce and Haldane, who argued it was "absolutely necessary" to offer cheap, efficient university education "if we are to keep pace with the artisans of Germany and France," it was passed with the aid of the Conservative party, the University's old enemy.[20] As if to still the doubts of the Association, one of its members, Arthur Rücker, was called from his post in the Royal College of Science to become the principal of the reconstructed university.

After the first partial achievement of reform of the University of London, reorganization of higher education in the provincial towns immediately followed. During the years when he was most alarmed by the international situation and was carrying the burden of the Boer conflict, Joseph Chamberlain founded the University of Birmingham. Interested all his life in education, his thinking had been directed toward university education in the eighties by the efforts of Ramsay and others to win support for the university colleges, and by a lecture, later printed as a pamphlet, delivered at Birmingham by J. R. Seeley in 1887. Chamberlain suggested the founding of provincial universities which were not to be copies of Oxford and Cambridge but designed on the model of the Scottish and German universities.[21] Mason's College in Birmingham had been chartered as a University College only in 1897 and that year Chamberlain had been elected Lord Rector of Glasgow University. His experience in Glasgow fortified his intention to create a university in Birmingham. Between then and July, 1901, he had obtained a charter for a University of Birmingham, and had raised with the help of others an endowment of £450,000, securing in addition a considerable annual income, partly from the rates of the municipality.[22]

Chamberlain's vision of the new university was, as might be expected, ambitious and comprehensive: it was to combine instruction in all the subjects of higher education from the humanities, fine arts, and the sciences, to the technical and commercial. A school of brewing was included, for example, as well as a school of commerce, headed by William Ashley. A contributor was Andrew Carnegie who coupled his gift of £50,000 for the sciences with a suggestion that a committee be sent to America to inspect the scientific schools. On their return, after expressing their admiration for the schools visited, they, too, marvelled how "Everywhere we found evidence that the wealthier citizens realise the importance of university education, and encourage the universities by generous gifts . . ."[23]

The most brilliant and tireless supporter of the extension of university education was Haldane. Long impressed with the educational efficiency of the German universities, he opposed the separation of science and of technology from the university. As in the University of London, seeking to bring within the same walls undergraduate colleges, art schools, science, medical, and technical institutions, he became the great exponent of the founding of what he himself named "civic universities." To all the cities with university colleges, as well as to many others, he gave invaluable encouragement to increase their educational offerings throughout these years until it seemed as if no opening of a new university or building was complete without his presence on the platform. In a characteristic address to the College of Liverpool in 1901 he too stressed the double purpose of education and the needs of the nation in view of German and American competition. Combined with this was an appeal to local feeling and a stimulation of municipal rivalry, all of which led to the founding of universities before 1914, not only in Liverpool but in other towns as well. That the eleven new universities founded in this period should first become "municipal service stations," as their historian has called them, was inevitable.[24] Universities are not built in a day even when funds are plentiful, and the civic universities were before the war always semi-starved financially, in spite of some occasional large gifts.

2.

Toward a secondary school system

The defeats in South Africa aroused both scholars and scientists as well as other men. A new educational ferment began which had as its basis the fear of Germany and of England's industrial "decay." The consular reports were widely publicized.[25] Lord Avebury, an old-fashioned Liberal who believed in the beneficence of international competition,[26] warned nevertheless of Britain's backwardness in technical education,[27] as did Lord Rosebery and Devonshire.[28] Sir Andrew Noble, armaments manufacturer, had already lamented "the very much greater comparative progress that Germany, the United States and Switzerland had made in machinery" due to "our seriously neglecting technical instruction."[29]

Karl Pearson took advantage of the "temporary awakening of the English people" by the events in South Africa to urge in *National Life from the Standpoint of Science* (1901) the necessity of better-trained minds and more education in science.[30] The part of his argument which attracted most attention unfortunately dealt with the fact that the struggle for existence between nations for territory, trade routes, manufacturing supremacy, and finally in war was a necessary condition of human progress. A disciple of Francis Galton, he warned of a decline in fitness of the British population due to an adulteration with the inferior blood of immigrants and to a relatively higher birthrate among the less fit elements of the people. *Nature* assigned two scientists to review the book. Ray Lankester supported Pearson's demand for better education, attacking the University of Oxford and the opposition to scientific education generally. But he denied any biological warrant for Pearson's belief that human progress depended upon continuous warfare between human societies.[31] John Perry, professor of mathematics at the Royal College of Science, had himself urged the need for the nation "to increase its brain-power" in *England's Neglect of Science* (1900). Noting that "every man of sense in the kingdom is fully alive to the fact that this struggle for existence is going on," he declared "there are many other things to be thought of, many things which Prof. Pearson's mere Aryan science cannot take into account." He recalled Huxley's and Lockyer's past pleas and insisted "Our cry is for education and only that; true education for everybody, from the highest to the lowest, is a national necessity more important than any weapon of war or any political machinery for the repression of bad stock, because education will give us all these things and much more."[32]

At the same time numerous demands for the promotion of research and original investigation were pressed. Michael Foster urged it in *Nineteenth Century*.[33] At the opening of the Royal College of Science and the University of London, W. A. Tilden spoke on the topic and though he declared himself one who did not willingly refer to Germany because of the "exaggerated nonsense often talked about German competition and English incompetence," he had to admit that "the universities of Germany have settled the question for us and all the rest of the world . . ."[34] At the University of Edinburgh Professor J. G. Macgregor contrasted the German and American university emphasis upon research with the conservative spirit in Great Britain which "has prevented the course of university development demanded by the requirements of the age."[35]

Ernest Henry Starling, physiologist of London University and with experience in a German university (Breslau), wrote on "The Pressing Need for More Universities," forcefully restating all the arguments so often used, and urging "the founding of universities in connection with our great industrial centres and the equipment of the nation for the war of the twentieth century." He continuously cited the example and the threat of Germany.[36] J. A. Fleming, professor of electrical engineering at University College, London, writing on how the Electric Lighting Act of 1882, by giving local authorities control over electric power, had hindered the manufacture of electric energy "in bulk," found the universities crippled by the inadequacies of primary and secondary education. "In the terrible contest for commercial supremacy with the United States and Germany, towards which this country is advancing, nothing will avail us unless the young men who are to be masters of works, foremen, heads of departments, and directors of industries based on applications of scientific knowledge, are equipped with the most thorough knowledge of the arts they direct."[37]

At the Glasgow meeting of the British Association in 1901 Percy Frankland returned to the fray in his address as president of the chemistry section. After pointing out that English chemists had only rarely studied at Oxford or Cambridge, and were indebted to Germany for their training, he declared, "The opening of the new century is in reality a year of very serious awakening to those Englishmen who are not deaf to the voices in the air around them.

It is rapidly dawning upon many that 'the greatest empire which the world has ever seen' cannot be maintained unless we cast off insular prejudices and traditions . . . It is being continually impressed upon us in the newspapers and dinned into our ears from every platform that it is imperative for this country to approximate more to German ideas and methods . . ."[38] The theme was continued by A. G. Green in one of the sectional papers, "The Coal-Tar Colour Industry in Germany and England," in which he documented Britain's loss to Germany of this ever-growing industry.[39]

All these writers, and many others, mentioned, if only in passing, the immediate need for reform of secondary education. Plans for such reform had been under consideration since the report of the Royal Commission of 1895 on Secondary Education. That Commission under the chairmanship of James Bryce had heard endless descriptions of the "confusion arising from lack of organisation," of the "over-lapping from over-supply," of the over-lapping from "higher school doing the work of lower."[40] After extended hearings, the Commission, guided by Michael Sadler and Bryce,[41] reported that in the internal organization of the secondary schools, the "foremost need is that secondary teachers should be systematically trained in the methods and practice of education,"[42] thus raising the old demand for professional preparation, so long resisted in every area of English life. The Commission also reported that there was "a remarkable consensus of opinion on this point:—That in order to constitute an efficient and satisfactory Central Authority there must be a Minister of Education, the head of a Department, responsible to Parliament, with a seat in the Cabinet, a Minister who, as Sir William Hart-Dyke said, would be a Secretary of State. On this matter witnesses of all orders, Charity Commissioners, Government officials, schoolmasters, representatives of local authorities, and statesmen were agreed. They were agreed, also, that as he was to be responsible he must be supreme, though his supremacy was not always heartily or willingly accepted."[43] Once again the demand for the state to assume authority in order to produce an orderly system of national education in the interest of national efficiency was recorded.

An Education Bill in 1898 had been roundly denounced as inadequate. Now the movement assumed the nature of a ground swell. Sir John Gorst of the newly established Board of Education (1899) addressed the newly founded Education Section of the British Association. Finding that secondary education was "too tied to the traditional literary side," he stressed also the inadequacy of the 'polytechnical' schools. "A few elementary lessons in short-hand and bookkeeping will not fit the British people to compete with Germany." Yet despite his contention that the need was for "a scientific conception of a National Education System," he was careful to insist that it was not in the national interest "to scatter broadcast a huge system of higher instruction for anyone who chooses to take advantage of it, however unfit to receive it."[44] Official opinion remained more concerned over the possible waste of funds than the waste of any undeveloped talent.

The next year the new prime minister, Arthur Balfour, finally introduced a Secondary Education bill. Much of the preparatory work, a delicate matter since the bill brought under public support the Church of England schools as well as the non-denominational schools, was conducted behind the scenes by Robert Morant,[45] a rising officer in the Education Department who had learned from experience in the East the use of bureaucratic and autocratic political manipulation. Despite reservations, those who felt that improvement in education must be obtained at any cost, such as Sidney Webb, who aided in drafting the bill, Haldane, Lockyer, and even Chamberlain, knowing what it might cost him in Dissenter support, backed the bill. "The abandonment of the Bill would, in our opinion," Lockyer wrote, "be a disaster to education in England . . . Secondary education includes technical education, and national progress depends more upon the coordination and extension of these higher stages than upon elementary instruction . . . What the country needs are masters and managers educated in the truest sense of the term, men with scientific training and sympathies, able to appreciate latent possibilities of industrial developments and anxious to encourage all work which aims at the advancement of knowledge. It is in students of this class that England is lamentably deficient as compared with Germany and the United States . . ."[46]

As in the seventies the Elementary Education bill had been a response to the pressure of foreign industrial competition, so too was the Secondary Education bill in 1902. But where the earlier bill had for its purpose to improve the preparation of the common workmen, the bill for secondary education had a broader intent: including the ablest working-class children, it was intended to prepare for higher education future technologists and masters of the workmen. The bill was bitterly attacked and resisted by the Dissenters, but their violent opposition was directed against the religious aspect of the bill rather than the public provision of education. Gradually the state was being compelled to recognize that in its own interests better informed and trained minds were required and for that, more than improved technical training was necessary. However, as a recent historian of English education wrote, even this Act of 1902 "did not go so far as to create a national system of education . . ."[47]

In the same year, while the debate was at its height over the Secondary Education bill, two publications appeared; Sadler's volume on *Secondary Education in Germany* and a Report of the Special Sub-committee on the Application of Science to Industry published by the Technical Education Board of the London County Council. Serious studies, based upon carefully collected evidence, both were widely read and alarmed many influential men.

Sadler's volume, in addition to its penetrating and balanced observations on German *Kultur*, was an elaborate and critical study of the German secondary schools, particularly in their broader implications for higher education. Noting the desire of certain German educational authorities to introduce something of the English spirit with its relative freedom from restraint into their own system, Sadler nonetheless made embarrassingly clear the insufficiency and inefficiency of British education in contrast to the German. He emphasized particularly the indifference of the English to hard intellectual endeavor, an indifference he found reflected in the failure of the state to provide any appropriate organization to stimulate such endeavor. He attributed the excellence of German technical education, of the German universities, and even of governmental administration from the level of the Empire to the municipality to the professionally operated and state-supported secondary schooling. The result of the German system was a more intellectually homogeneous society in which educated men and experts were respected not only by scholars and scientists but by the whole community and, significantly, by the business men who eagerly sought their services. Approvingly, he quoted from a *Times* comment upon one of the Kaiser's speeches.

"What we have to face today is not the old competition in which Englishmen always held their own—the competition of individual with individual. We have to deal with a nation intellectually organised in such a fashion that the individual, though depending upon his own efforts, is in the position of a scout who has his supports to fall back upon and a staff to provide him with information."[48]

Like Balfour and Haldane, Sadler was a philosophical idealist, and he, too, insisted that "All true education has a double purpose, namely (1), the development of the moral personality, physical powers and intellectual gifts of the individual as individual, and (2) the fitting of the pupil skillfully to perform the duties of some special calling in life, and worthily to discharge the tasks likely to fall on him or her as a member of the community."[49]

The Report of the Technical Education Board might have been a complement to the Sadler volume, so aptly did it appear to drive home the lessons elaborated in the latter. Sidney Webb had served as chairman of the Committee making the investigation. The Committee consulted some two hundred expert witnesses, including the president and past-presidents of the Society of Chemical Industry.

The members studied some sixteen books, articles, and pamphlets, many of which have already been referred to, including the report of the Manchester Committee to Germany, and Sadler's volume. In their report, the Committee discussed both the "Loss of business" and the "Causes of loss." English manufacturers, they found, had "fallen seriously behind their foreign rivals . . . in no small degree [due] to the superior scientific education provided in foreign countries."[50] Again the loss to Germany of the synthetic dye industry was rehearsed and the loss of pharmaceutical manufactures. The great advances made in the manufacture of optical glass by the Germans was also noted, an advance largely attributed to scientific experiments subsidized by the German government. As a result the "manufacture of high-class lenses for photographic cameras, microscopes, telescopes, and field-glasses, as well as thermometer-glass tube for making thermometers for accurate physical measurements, has been practically lost to this country."[51] They noted the more rapid progress in the manufacture of electrical machinery in the United States, Germany, and Switzerland, and the rise in the value of British imports of electrical apparatus, including dynamos from Germany. Pottery manufacture was studied and had improved in America and Germany, and both Holland and Germany were increasing their exports of beer due to improvements resulting from scientific research. The witnesses "were practically all agreed in considering" the relative backwardness in England as due "to the deficiencies of our educational system."[52]

The Sadler volume and the Report of the Technical Education Board, appearing at a moment of intense concern with the German rivalry, set off one of the great campaigns in England for reform of education in science and technology. The campaign was expressly designed to meet the German competition in every form, and though the United States and other countries were often referred to, it was Germany with which the reformers were almost obsessed.

3.

A London "Charlottenburg" and Lockyer's campaign

Haldane brought the two works to the attention of certain of his wealthy friends.[53] The following year Lord Rosebery, long active in the London County Council, as Chancellor of London University addressed a letter to Lord Monkswell, chairman of the Council, as the authority for technical education in the city.[54] After noting the Technical Education Board's Report on the inadequacy of provision for advanced instruction in scientific technology and original research in London compared with "perhaps the most perfect instance of such provision . . . the great College of Applied Science at Charlottenburg," he proposed the founding of a "London 'Charlottenburg'." Wernher, Beit & Co. had offered £100,000 to a body of trustees and other offers would be forthcoming. He had agreed to act as chairman; other trustees were to include the

Duke of Devonshire, Arthur Balfour, Francis Mowatt, Julius Wernher, R. B. Haldane, the Vice-Chancellor, and the Principal of London University. Would the representatives of the London County Council act with them? Shortly afterwards, the Board of Education appointed a departmental commission with Haldane as Chairman to work out specific proposals. The result of several years' work was the founding of the Imperial College of Science with King Edward laying the cornerstone in 1909.[55] In the new institution, which was made part of the University of London, were fused the Royal College of Science, the Royal College of Mines, and the Central Technical College. The state provided an annual income of £20,000 as did the London County Council. Subsequently, Ernest Cassell and the Rothschilds contributed; Wernher, Beit & Co. doubled their original gift, and Alfred Beit bequeathed to it £125,000.[56]

Other movements were set afoot by Norman Lockyer. In preparation for his presidential address to the British Association in 1903, he printed a series of essays in *Nature* under the title, "The University in the Modern State." Written by himself and others, the articles stressed the role of governments, particularly the German, in developing "brain-power," offering a wealth of information on the scientific foundations abroad. The title of his address was "The Influence of Brain-power on History," obviously adapted from Mahan, and returning to his earlier comparison of science and sea-power.[57] For forcefulness, the address can only be compared with Playfair's of eighteen years before.

Reviewing at length the conditions of the contemporary world, he pointed out the importance of science in relation to them, quoting Balfour, Chamberlain, and Rosebery on the need for more and better universities for the promotion of science and scientific research. Citing the cost of the German universities to the state and estimating what it would cost Britain to equal them, he referred to the enormous and necessary expenditures on the Navy in order to maintain a two-power standard. "How then," he inquired, "do we stand with regard to universities, recognising them as the chief producers of brain-power and therefore the equivalent of battleships in relation to sea-power? . . . instead of having universities equalling in number those of two [Germany and the

United States] of our chief competitors together, they are by no means equal to those of either of them singly . . . The pity is that our Government has considered sea-power alone; that while so completely guarding our commerce, it has given no thought to one of the main conditions on which its production and increase depend; a glance could have shown that other countries were building universities even faster than they were building battle-ships; were, in fact, considering brainpower first and sea-power afterwards." The country needed at least eight new universities which would cost about £24,000,000. Turning to the subject of the encouragement of research, and reviewing what had been done, Lockyer reminded his hearers of the need for a scientific council, proposed so long before by the Devonshire Commission, and such as Lord Curzon had instituted in India, and as the Germans already had. In the meantime, he called for the scientists and educators of the nation to create an organization, whether a committee of the British Association or some other society, to urge continuously "that we shall be armed as other nations are with efficient universities and facilities for research . . ."

The address was followed up by further action. Assisted by a committee of the British Association, consisting of the Deputy Vice-Chancellor of the University of Oxford, the Vice-Chancellor of the University of Cambridge, the Principal of the University of Birmingham, Oliver Lodge, Michael Foster, and Henry Roscoe, Lockyer drew up a formal statement on the lines of his address.[58] Reinforced by a delegation numbering four hundred, representing science, scholarship, and nearly every institution associated with those interests in the Empire, the Committee called upon the Government in person. They were received by Balfour and Austen Chamberlain who recognized the importance of such a very large group of distinguished men. Having listened to the prepared statement, the Prime Minister admitted the backwardness of Britain in comparison to Germany but urged that the capitalists required first to be convinced of the need of the science-educated man. Chamberlain, Chancellor of the Exchequer, reported that as a result of Lockyer's address an additional grant had been given to the university colleges and he hoped to be able to double it the following year. He then raised the pertinent delaying questions:

"if the universities would consider to what extent they are willing to come under control if they receive grants, to what extent the State is to have a voice in fixing the fees of students, to what extent it is to direct or influence the teaching, whether it is to allocate its assistance to promote special branches of study, or whether it is desired to make every university complete in itself."[59]

The demand for state assistance to the universities embodied in fact a more radical proposal than the provision of state assistance to elementary or secondary education. The industrial competition had with the advance of technology awakened many to the necessity of providing for the lower schools. Beyond that point education was regarded, in what was still a society with marked class distinctions, as a prerogative of the aristocracy, who by definition did not work with their hands. Even surgery was only beginning to gain status, while the chemist, physicist, and engineer were regarded as superior kinds of laborers. The aristocracy's tenaciously held belief that all other classes generally lacked the ability to profit by higher education—and that meant the Public Schools, Oxford, and Cambridge—remained untouched by the obvious fact that many of their own class also revealed little evidence of such ability.

Nor did the business climate favor the reformers. Business in general did not seem to be falling off. Exports and imports continued to rise and trade balances remained favorable. Most businessmen and politicians were unable to see how the advancing technologies were gradually rendering obsolete not only the practices but the plants and the manpower of the British economy. Only the exceptionally farsighted or those engaged in the more technical industries joined the scientists and scholars in their efforts to alter the foundations of British life in order to prepare for war or against the day when cotton textiles, coal, ship-building, and foreign loans would no longer maintain their economy in a healthy condition. As late as 1914, except for the few, the day of reckoning seemed far off, if indeed there was to be such a day. As Balfour said, they needed to be persuaded.

Accordingly, in October, 1905, at a large meeting held at the Mansion House and presided over by the Lord Mayor, the British Science Guild was founded to promote Lockyer's proposals and to produce the needed persuasion. As Lockyer pointed out in the report of the organizing committee: "It was a question of conducting all our national activities, State service, private service, and what not, under the best possible conditions with the greatest amount of brain-power."[60] The British Science Guild, like so many such groups at the time, had for its purpose the promotion of national efficiency, and its founders constituted a distinguished roster.[61]

The Bishop of Ripon, nominating Haldane for president, observed according to the report in the *Times* that "Our manufacturers, and perhaps our farmers, had been content to go on in what might be called jogtrot ways . . . the mere rule of thumb and the traditional methods had prevailed . . . Those things were precisely the way in which that Science Guild might come forward and do what had been done in Germany . . ." Sir William Mather of the engineering firm of Mather and Platt, supporting the motion, said: "We knew what the Germans knew, and what the Americans knew. The trouble was that the people of England had not been trained to enable them to use largely the methods of science and the principles of science which the people of other countries— not the select men, not the men specifically gifted . . . but the men who had the conduct, even in subordinate positions, of some of the departments of scientific manufacture possessed." Haldane in his acceptance address agreed that "We had to see how we could get the German faculty of organisation, train people to think more of it, and apply it to the various departments of our affairs."[61a]

From the date of its founding the British Science Guild pursued the intention of its founders, and it continued to grow. By 1912 its membership numbered about 900. It received much of the credit for bringing about the founding by the Government in 1909 of the Development Commission for Agriculture and Woodlands.[62] But it had not limited its interests to Britain. At the time of the Colonial Ministers Conference in 1907 the Guild joined with the British Empire League to pay honor to the visitors. Speaking for the colonial ministers in reply to the toasts, Alfred Deakin of Australia observed that the Empire "needs method, principle and organization" but that they were "three things we seem incapable of introducing into our Empire."[63] To accomplish these aims was part of the Guild's purpose.

Despite Austen Chamberlain's undertaking, in no year before the war was the government grant to the colleges doubled, though it was gradually increased. In 1907 it was announced that a limit was being set on aid to university colleges at £100,000 per annum and £10,000 to any one of them. Newspaper discussion followed. The *Morning Post* noted that "Berlin does not limit its government grant to university and other forms of higher education to any such sum . . ." Mr. Asquith knew as well as any one else "how many millions such men as Sir Robert Giffen and Sir Norman Lockyer think the British Government will have to spend on universities and colleges if England is to keep her place among the nations." *Nature* presented a table showing a fifty per cent increase in annual grants to the German universities from 1891–2 to 1906. "Unless our statesmen can be made to realise the supreme importance of this matter . . . we must reconcile ourselves to the idea that as a manufacturing and distributing people we shall in due course have to occupy a third or fourth place among the nations of the world."[64] By 1914 the grants had risen to £170,000, a notable increase from the £15,000 of 25 years before but still barely enough to enable many of the universities to keep their doors open.[65] Nevertheless, both the existence of more universities and the increase in grants were due in large measure to the German competition and the German example.

4.

The old universities and the internationalization of learning

As usual, when British education was being criticized, Oxford and Cambridge came under attack. Even before Lockyer had begun his campaign, James Dewar, having testified before the Technical Education Committee, delivered in the fall of 1902 his address as President of the British Association on the theme of "The Endowment of Education." He noted that "Our exceptional men have too often worked in obscurity, without recognition from a public too imperfectly instructed to guess at their greatness, without assistance from a State governed largely by dialecticians, and without help from academic authorities hidebound by the pedantries of medieval scholasticism." As an example of the neglect of science he cited the Royal British Institution, finding that the total expenditure, including salaries, administration and facilities of that famous scientific center "during the whole of the nineteenth century . . . comes to £119,800, or an average of £1,200 per annum." The loss of the chemical industries was not due to a lax patent law, as some maintained, but to want of education. "To my mind, the really appalling thing is not that the Germans have seized this or that other industry . . . It is that the German population has reached a point of general training and specialised equipment which it will take us two generations of hard and intelligently directed educational work to attain. It is that Germany possesses a national weapon of precision which must give her an enormous initial advantage in any and every contest depending upon disciplined and methodised intellect."[66]

Such indirect criticism of the educational Establishment was not enough, however; this time the charges against the ancient universities were to be brought directly home to them. The following year the secretaries of the Royal Society addressed a letter to the universities, directing attention to a resolution adopted by the President and Council of the Society: "That the universities be respectfully urged to consider the desirability of taking such steps in respect of their regulations as will, as far as possible, ensure that a knowledge of science is recognised in schools and elsewhere as an essential part of education."[67] And to aid Lockyer's campaign, John Perry at a public meeting in Oxford attacked that University not merely for neglecting science, but for being "its active enemy pretending friendship." The contributions made in its earlier years to science were among its greatest glories, but modern Oxford was largely responsible for the misconception of what a university education really means.[68]

The following year William Huggins in his presidential address to the Royal Society broadened the attack. "In my opinion," he said, "the scientific deadness of the nation is mainly due to the too exclusively medieval and classical methods of our higher public schools."[69]

Efforts to remove compulsory Greek from the examinations had been defeated by a small margin of votes at both the old universities. The question had been raised by the scientists and those interested in welcoming students from abroad. Oxford did not recognize any degrees from other universities except those of Cambridge, Edinburgh, and Dublin as exempting students from the undergraduate requirements, which included Greek for responsions.

Cambridge had, however, in 1895 adopted a policy of accepting students with degrees from other universities, subject to approval by a committee, as research students, thus freeing them from the undergraduate requirements. At first such students were simply to be candidates for the B. A. or the M. A., but shortly they were admitted as candidates for the doctorate. At Cambridge Rayleigh and J. J. Thomson had built up a great physics department, and schools of engineering, agriculture, and forestry were being founded; they were prepared to offer advanced degrees particularly in the sciences.[70]

Oxford also instituted the research degrees of Baccalaureate and Doctorate of Letters and Science, though without altering the old requirements for foreign students. However, as late as 1903 there were at Oxford, according to the classical archaeologist Percy Gardner, neither "the seminar nor such advanced study" as was required for graduate work. "In fact," he wrote, "in relation to research Oxford stands where the universities of France and America stood thirty years ago," while with the German universities no comparison was possible.[71] In 1904 C. H. Firth in his inaugural address as Regius Professor of History brought down upon himself the wrath of the dons by calling attention to the lack of professional training in research in history at Oxford. Only during the first decade of the new century were schools for final honors in English language and literature and in modern languages, other than as philological or linguistic studies, being slowly developed there.[72] Nevertheless the doctoral degree was instituted, principally, however, to enable foreign students to compete with the German doctorates. Except in the sciences, English students continued to regard the degree with marked condescension.[73]

For reasons neither the Royal Society nor the dons foresaw, changes were in the making, however. Not only were the demands of the State to exceed all expectations in the near future, but the

colleges of the two ancient universities, long so wealthy and so
spendthrift of their endowments, were to be forced to appeal
publicly for financial aid. As early as 1897 the Duke of Devonshire, as Chancellor of the University of Cambridge, called public
attention to the financial difficulties of the University. Two years
later a Cambridge University Association was formed to collect
funds. They found that the professors and all other instructors
were inadequately paid and "the University can set aside only
£200 per annum to form a pension fund for its forty-four professors, and nothing at all for other teachers."[74] In 1902 Oxford
issued a "Statement of the Needs of the University." In 1905 a
more formal and public appeal was made in which the University's needs were set forth in detail with requests for contributions
both for immediate capital outlay and for investment. The appeal
bore the signatures of forty-three professors, readers, and curators,
the majority being among the German-influenced reformers and
the scientists.[75] Two years later Cambridge appealed for a million
and a half pounds and Oxford sought at least a quarter of a million.

In making the last appeal for Cambridge, the Duke of Devonshire revealed that during the preceding seven years the efforts
of the Cambridge University Association had resulted in the collection of £16,000. *Nature* calculated that at the same rate it
would require more than ninety years to collect the sum the University now required, and noted that Oxford had been no more
successful in appealing to private sources. "The fact is, if we are
to rely entirely upon private generosity to secure for this country
the advantages of an adequate number of universities, planned,
equipped, and financed on a scale liberal enough to meet modern
needs, our chances of obtaining a supply of places of higher education comparable with that in Germany and the United States,
are small indeed." To re-enforce the argument, the expenditures
of the United States and Germany were again set forth.[76]

In 1907, Bishop Gore of Birmingham proposed the appointment
of a Royal Commission "to inquire into the endowment, government, administration, and teaching of the Universities . . . in
order to secure the best uses of their resources for all classes of
the community." The Bishop of Bristol opposed, concluding, however, that Cambridge would welcome a statutory commission which

could "cut some knots which the University could not, or would not, cut for itself. One of these questions was Greek."[77] The Government asked for time to consider, while the Oxford reformers, though they found their own efforts blocked within the University, hurried a counterproposal into the columns of the *Times* because they did not relish reform by the Birmingham bishop.[78]

The same year that he was deprecating a royal commission for Oxford, the Vice-Chancellor T. H. Warren, speaking on behalf of the British Science Guild at the banquet for the colonial ministers, declared that the old universities "realise that they are not only universities of a kingdom, but universities of an Empire," a statement which had at least the merit of foreshadowing the establishment of an Imperial University Bureau as urged by George Parkin, the strong advocate of imperial federation and administrator for the Rhodes Scholarship Trustees, in 1912.[79] But if the institutional changes were few at Oxford and Cambridge, despite Curzon's stirring of the waters at the former during the last years of his chancellorship,[80] the old exclusiveness in the world of scholarship as well as in science was passing away.

International institutionalization of scholarship and science had been initiated by the Academies of Munich, Leipzig, and Göttingen, forming with the Academy of Vienna "a cartel". Arthur Schüster, physics professor at Owens College, Manchester, trained at Heidelberg, heard of this development on a visit to Germany. He sought to interest the Royal Society in this collaboration for the promotion of learning and won its consent to his attending a meeting of the cartel at Leipzig in 1897.[81] To the meeting at Göttingen the next year the Society also sent its two secretaries, Michael Foster and Arthur Rücker. The representatives of the Royal Society were impressed with the possibilities of joint activity but insisted that the proposed organization be made truly international by inviting the academies of Paris and of St. Petersburg to be members. In 1899 at Wiesbaden, statutes were drawn up for an International Association of Academies.

The Royal Society did not, however, include—as many of the foreign academies did—the historical, philosophical, and philological disciplines, nor was there in England any general society for those studies. Schüster and Lockyer, among others, advocated expansion by the Royal Society to include them. But the Society refused. The result was the founding in 1902 of the British Academy for the Promotion of Historical, Philosophical, and Philological Studies.[82] Dicey, who opposed all collective enterprises, criticized the membership as self-elected and unrepresentative.[83] That was unfair and in part, at least, untrue since the initial members of the Council included: W. R. Anson, Ingram Bywater, Rhys Davids, S. R. Driver, C. P. Ilbert, R. C. Jebb, J. E. B. Mayor, H. F. Pelham, W. W. Skeat, A. W. Ward, James Ward, and James Bryce.[84] The presence of many German-influenced scholars was fitting for an organization created under such auspices.

Although the new Academy was founded and the International Association of Academies continued to meet until the outbreak of war in 1914, the study of the humanities was little affected in England. As A. F. Pollard was to note in 1920, although the original sources for study of the history of the English-speaking peoples were available only in London, most even "of those students went before the War to Berlin or other German Universities or to Paris," because no English university had "made adequate progress in specialisation for the post-graduate study of historical, political, and legal science."[85]

5.

Plans for technical and medical educational reform

A renewed interest in technical education, increasingly distinguished from technological instruction at the university level, followed the publication of *Continuation Schools in England and Elsewhere* in 1907 by M. E. Sadler. The continuation school was introduced as part of the general movement for social reform in the interest of efficiency. The consequences led to a concern for young people who, as half-timers, began to work at twelve years of age. Replaced in their jobs when they reached adulthood by other children, they remained thereafter often unemployable as a result of lack of skills. As earlier, the movement was also related to the decay of the old apprenticeship system with the coming of more technical requirements. Sadler furnished details of the laws governing the employment of children in Britain, Germany, and

Switzerland, and the evidence revealed that the half-timer suffered actual physical, as well as mental and moral, deterioration. J. Wertheimer of Bristol University College, reviewing Sadler's book, compared the difference between the continuation schools of Germany, which had for the most part abolished evening classes, with the predominance of evening schools in England. The disadvantages of evening classes after a long day of work were clearly set forth in Sadler's volume, as they were to be again in later studies. The same disadvantages were found to exist in the technological training in the English civic universities.[86]

A campaign was begun to abolish half-timers by making continuation schools compulsory, "as in Germany." The British Science Guild's Education Committee and the Higher Education Subcommittee of the London County Council's Education Committee proposed various plans, and the usual "influential delegation" waited upon the Prime Minister. As usual, also, he was agreeable, but raised objections.[87] Thereafter the subject was under continuous discussion. In January of 1910 Sadler again noted "the keener interest on the part of the mass of German employers in educational questions, and especially in the educational aspect of the daily duties of the workshop." But he cautioned, as had Haldane, against overenthusiasm in imitating the Germans. "We in England have indeed much to learn from Germany . . . but it is right to remember that, for historical reasons which are far from discreditable to us, we have approached the problem from the point of view of the individual rather than from the point of view of the State . . . I would venture to urge that our task is so to use the collective power of the State as to stimulate, but not to supersede, the energy and forethought of the individual. Bureaucratic collectivism in education seems to me as false an ideal as, at the opposite extreme, is chaotic and plunging individualism."[88] Perceptive and judicious as this statement was, it may also have tended to confirm many employers in their indifference.

By that time the London County Council and the Science Guild had increased the tempo and urgency of their campaign. R. Blair, the former's executive officer, asked the British consul in Berlin, Dr. Frederick Rose, to make a comparison of the training of students in the German technical high schools and in the British universities and technical institutions of university rank. Rose, a German, concluded his detailed study by observing rather patronizingly that the English polytechnics represented "a stage of development which German technical schools passed through about forty years ago . . ." Matriculation at German technical universities required completion of the full nine-year secondary school course at a classical, semi-classical or modern secondary school; this, he believed, was practically equivalent to a B. A. pass degree at Oxford or Cambridge. Commenting on Rose's memorandum, Blair wrote that "taking, as far as one can, comparable institutions, there are 12,000 fully qualified students attending day institutions for the highest technical training in Germany and only about 3,600 in the United Kingdom. The German courses are, speaking generally, longer and the previous preparation better." This was "because the German people believe in the application of trained intelligence to all forms of national activity."[89]

The report gave further impetus to the work of the British Science Guild. The subject was discussed by Arthur Smithells, himself trained in Germany, in his presidential address to the Society of British Gas Industries in 1911.[90] In the House of Commons, Walter Runciman, president of the Board of Education, reviewing the work of the year, concluded that "When one records all, there is still left the feeling that in England there is not full appreciation of higher technological work, and when we make comparison of the number of students at German and English universities it is all to the advantage of Germany and not to our credit. In the eleven modern universities of England at the present time full-time students number 9,600, and if you add 7,000 at Oxford and Cambridge of under- and post-graduates, you have a total for England and Wales of 16,600 students. It sounds like a large number, but when you remember that Germany has 63,000 students in similar institutions, we may well say we have a long journey before us."[91] That some further reservations might be needed by the computation is suggested by a report of the Advisory Committee on University Grants the next year. Out of 22,000 students in the institutions assisted, only 3,000 had reached or passed the third year, and "the great disproportion between the volume of true University work and that of other work" was so great as to "distort the conception of what a university education should be."[92]

This picture was re-enforced by the evidence presented before the Royal Commission on University Education in London (1909–1912). A committee was appointed to study again the relations of the various schools forming that University, largely as a result of the new Imperial College's desire to achieve independent status. Its chairman was the untiring Haldane, and among the members were Milner, Robert Morant of the Education Office, and the widow of Bishop Creighton. The evidence again brought out the difficulties in advanced education resulting from the inadequacies of elementary and secondary education. Of special interest as an example of the German influence, in this case mediated by the American, was medical education.

No institutions better than the medical schools and hospitals of London exemplified all that was best and most characteristic of traditional English institutions and, by their resistance to change, the failure to adjust to the development of science and scientific technology. The principal medical schools of London were attached to eleven large general hospitals. Although some of these took paying patients in special wards, they were in general charity hospitals devoted to the care of the indigent sick. Served by the most famous London physicians without salary, supported by endowment, by donations from their lay governors and by public charity, they were monuments to English philanthropy. Their patients received the best care given anywhere in the world and until the last quarter of the nineteenth century both the hospitals and their medical schools were justly famous as models of excellence. The schools, which developed from the practice of students walking the wards with physicians, were the property of the hospital physicians.

The usual means of becoming a famous consulting physician—the Harley Street mark of success—was to enter the medical school and, after finishing the training course, to accept whatever minor and poorly paid post might be available in the school or hospital. Seniority prevailed and advancement, though slow, was reasonably certain. It meant poverty and hard work for many years and the luxury of a great practice afterwards. For once established as a hospital physician, only a few hours of the day need be spent making the rounds of the wards with the residents and students and the rest to a lucrative consulting practice which followed from the appointment. The educational excellence of the English system lay in the practical, bedside teaching with its empirical observation of and interest in the individual patient. Both the hospitals and medical schools exhibited the English preference for private, voluntary or amateur administration, their strong philanthropic impulses, their care for the individual, the empirical, observational approach to study, and the older apprenticeship method of learning.

As the sciences of physiology, biology, chemistry, and physics began to make their contributions to medicine, attempts were gradually made to meet the new conditions in the medical schools. Training in the sciences was introduced by the addition of laboratories and the hiring of men to teach in them. Since this meant additional expense, however, the laboratories remained small and poorly equipped, the sciences were taught by anyone who would accept the positions, and the instruction was mostly elementary. Study of the sciences and laboratory research were regarded as supplements to education rather than contributions to the principal work of curing patients. A few men worked in the laboratories, but usually only until they went into private practice or secured a better paid position in the hospital. Partly as a consequence of this situation in the hospital schools and partly due to the backwardness of the development of scientific technology in other English schools, which the hospital schools simply reflected, the scientific treatment of disease, associated with physiological and pathological investigation, lagged behind the Continent and particularly behind Germany.[93]

As early as 1835 James Paget, who was to become one of England's greatest physicians, was advised to study German and believed it was the most important step in his career because of the tremendous advantage which familiarity with German research gave him over his fellows.[94] Going to Germany to study medicine became almost common practice. English students of medicine, seeking to become specialists, we are told, "often worked in a foreign country, which in the latter part of the century meant Germany," and "in fact the future was open to, and was made by, the men" who did.[95]

The great change in medicine introduced by the development of bacteriology in the seventies and eighties, if begun by Frenchmen, was vigorously and most successfully prosecuted by the Germans under the leadership of Robert Koch. Many of the Englishmen who took up bacteriology had worked under Koch himself, as had C. T. Roy, professor of pathology at Cambridge (1884–1897); A. A. Kanthack, Director of Pathology at St. Bartholomew's Hospital and briefly professor of the same subject at Cambridge; his successor at Cambridge, the Edinburgh man G. Sims Woodhead, founder of the *Journal of Pathology and Bacteriology* (1893);[96] David Bruce and his wife;[97] and William Watson Cheyne, Lister's disciple and translator of Koch.[98] English bacteriologists had studied in other German physiological and pathological laboratories, as had E. Klein of University College and St. Bartholomew's,[99] or G. H. F. Nuttall of Oxford,[100] and they in turn encouraged and influenced the younger men such as Ronald Ross.[101]

In like manner the scientific study of hygiene, originating largely in the work of English sanitarians, was systematized and elaborated into a modern discipline by the Germans, Max von Pettenkofer, Rudolf Virchow, and others. Greatly altered by advances in bacteriology, hygiene returned as a scientific discipline to England through Nuttall, an American, who had studied not only at the University of California and the Johns Hopkins, but at Breslau, Göttingen, and the Berlin Hygienic Institute. Nuttall, brought from Germany to Oxford in 1900 by Clifford Allbut, Regius Professor of Physics, became Quick Professor of Biology in 1906 and the founder and editor of the *Journal of Hygiene* in 1900 and *Parisitology* in 1908.[102]

Lister's great work itself underwent a similar metamorphosis. An empirical investigator, like his co-religionist Edward Tylor, Lister perfected his antiseptic method of surgery with its carbolic spray after learning of Pasteur's work. Ignored or ridiculed by the majority of English surgeons, the antiseptic method was quickly taken up by the Germans. On its foundations the German surgeon, E. G. B. von Bergmann, developed a system of aseptic surgery. The immaculate, aseptic operating theaters of the present day have developed from what von Bergmann himself described as a "critical repetition and improvement" on Lister's antiseptic surgery.[103] The English adopted the new system from Germany.[104]

That the English medical schools were unsatisfactory was an

old complaint; as early as the Royal Commission of 1884, and more frequently before the Lords Committee on the Metropolitan Hospitals in 1891, both the Scottish and German practices were cited as superior to the English. Widespread discontent with English medical education and practice arose only after 1900. The older criticisms were repeated: the variety of portals by which entry into medical practice was obtainable; the different requirements of Scottish versus London degrees; the rigid promotion by seniority within the hospitals. These had long been subjects of debate. The new criticism centered on the overcrowding of the medical curriculum, the lack of scientific technology applied in both medical teaching and practice, the need of greater specialization, and particularly the failure to encourage research in men beyond the conventional student age. At the same time, ambitious young men were finding other ways to a consulting practice than through appointment to the hospitals; they were making their names known by publishing in the various scientific, technological, and medical journals.

This might have meant nothing, however, had William Osler not accepted appointment as Regius Professor of Medicine at Oxford in 1905. Osler, Canadian-born and trained, had studied with Burdon-Sanderson and E. Klein in the physiological laboratory of University College, London, becoming fully acquainted with English medical and hospital practices before going to study in Berlin and Vienna. His career took him to McGill University, Montreal, the University of Pennsylvania, and to the Johns Hopkins University. In all three, he was active in medical research and in reforming medical education on the basis of his experience and knowledge of both English and German institutions. His appointment to Oxford ended his medical research; Osler himself is quoted as saying that there was no place like Oxford for a man who has passed his most strenuous years and wants to combine occupation with enjoyment.[105] His principal professional service in England was his support in behalf of public health and the reform of medical education and hospital organization.

In October 1909 Osler delivered two lectures at London Hospital in which he launched a vigorous attack upon British medical schools for their neglect of laboratory studies and facilities. Research and study should be cultivated without thought of examinations. This could only be done when the medical schools were provided with clinical wards and the teaching was in the hands of scientific investigators who were professors in the universities. It was the union of the hospitals and universities which gave Germany such great advantages. Though the students there did not receive bedside teaching as early, and were in this respect at a decided disadvantage, even when English hospitals were associated with colleges or universities as in the city colleges, the doctors did not control the beds in the infirmaries and were too often, as in London, primarily engaged in almost full-time practice. Medical and surgical clinics were required for modern medical education and this meant that the hospital schools must become parts of the universities.[106]

Shortly after, Abraham Flexner arrived in England. He was engaged in a study of Continental and British medical education on behalf of the Carnegie Foundation of New York for which he had recently completed an epoch-making survey of American medical schools, printed by the Foundation as its "Bulletin Number Four." This publication was already known to a few leading Englishmen through the offices of Nicholas Murray Butler of Columbia University.[107] Flexner, a graduate of the Johns Hopkins University, was well-known to Osler who introduced him to many of the leading figures in the medical and educational world of England. As a result he was invited to serve as witness before the Haldane Commission. His testimony, followed by that of Osler, and Max Müller of Munich, one of the most famous clinical professors of his day, and by such English physicians as Henry Head, Charles Sherrington, E. H. Starling, and many others who had either studied in German clinics or studied German medical education, resulted in the Commission's Report wholly supporting their proposals.[108]

The contrasts existing between the British and German systems of medical instruction were simply and clearly stated by Head in his testimony. He began by describing the British empirical method.

> The aim of all good clinical teaching is to start from the patient and to generalise from him; all good clinical teaching remains essentially teaching on a patient. It is the human

being, the patient before you, that is the subject, and if in the end you arrive at general principles you do so by starting from the point of the pyramid, diverging outwards to the generalisation. I know nowhere where that class of teaching is so excellently carried out as in the United Kingdom. That is the kind of teaching in which we excel . . . But the student requires not only this form of teaching . . . but also another class of teaching. He should know that he is coming to hear about the disease, *tabes dorsalis*, and he should find prepared for clinical demonstration a number of patients, each of whom is not interesting in himself but only interesting in that he exemplifies one particular aspect of the disease . . . The patients that are collected for such a demonstration are not then taken up from the point of view of the actual individual, but they are instances of a general condition; that is to say, the teacher starts with a general statement of the phenomena of the disease and comes down to particular instances. Now, that form of teaching requires an enormous amount of time for preparation . . . A man in active practice . . . cannot give the time necessary . . . as university teachers you must have men whose primary object in life is to give coordinate teaching. Such teaching a student must have if he is to keep abreast with knowledge, and such teaching can only be given by a man who has ample assistance and who devotes his time to the work . . . if a man is to be educated in a university manner, he must be taught to think generally. He must be taught to think according to principle, and not according to instances.[109]

As all the reformers noted, the English hospitals gave their best attention to the individual patient to the exclusion of the patient as an example of a particular disease; on the other hand, the Germans neglected the patient as an individual in their interest in the principle exemplified by particular instances. All the reformers insisted repeatedly on the need for combining the two approaches in the medical schools. Flexner was in many respects as critical of the German system as of the English. In Germany, due to the failure to maintain an adequate number of instructors and the monopoly by the professors *ordinarii* of the required courses, mass teaching by lecture with the demonstration method prevailed.[110] The result was that the student never came into contact with a patient until the end of his course when he entered into residency. But in respect to the advancement of the science of medicine the German had all the advantage. It was a combination of bedside instruction with full-time professional research scientists as clinical instructors that the reformers were urging.

That such a change in England would be enormously expensive to effect was granted; as in other matters, the old arrangement would have to be broken up to achieve the new order. The hospitals would have to be reorganized. Patients would have to be segregated according to the disease from which they suffered. The teachers would have to be university professors, men who were willing to devote their lives almost exclusively to research and teaching and to forego the possibility of large lucrative practices. New and more adequate laboratories would be required. But this, reformers insisted also, was the only way by which British medical and surgical practice and British medical education and research could be brought again into the first rank.

It was pointed out once more that medical education could not advance as long as it was based on inadequate general education. The British medical curriculum was cluttered up, whether in the London or provincial schools, with elementary courses in the sciences. Only by requiring such courses for admission, as the Johns Hopkins, the University Medical School of Washington University in St. Louis, and a handful of other university schools in the United States were doing, and as the German universities had long required, could a proper medical curriculum be established. As Henry S. Pritchett noted in his introduction to Flexner's report, "the most striking fact that emerges from this study is the absolute dependence of professional teaching in medicine upon the general educational system of the country itself. If one admits that professional education is primarily a question of education [rather than of medicine] this result must necessarily follow . . . One nation after another has undertaken to erect its professional schools upon the frailest foundations of general education. It is not too much to say that in every such instance the result has been a failure . . . in those countries in which the elementary and secondary school system is weak, the general level of professional education is low . . . Of the soundness of this conclusion there can be no more striking example than is furnished by a comparison between Germany on the one hand and the United States and England on the other. For the general high level of German professional training the German secondary school is mainly responsible."[111]

The Royal Commission in its report urged among other things the creation of medical and surgical units within the hospitals to be placed under the care of university professors as a way of introducing the German-American reforms advocated.[112] In addition, the Commission's hearings, combined with the reports of the Education Department, led Haldane to an important decision.

Despite his great work for education, Haldane had insisted, while a member of the Government, that the need for further funds for education had to be demonstrated before the Government could do more. The year following the Commission's final report, he announced at the Manchester Reform Club that after consultations with the Prime Minister, the Chancellor of the Exchequer, and Mr. Pease, Minister of Education, they had concluded that the "most urgent of the great social problems" was education. "The state of education in this country—elementary, secondary, and higher—is chaotic, and my colleagues and I feel the time has come when a step forward must be taken and on no small scale."[113] This was heartening to the reformers. R. A. Gregory noted that "among the developments adumbrated are the raising of the leaving age of compulsory attendance at primary schools, the abolition of the 'half-time' system, compulsory attendance at continuation schools, the correlation of primary and secondary schools, improvement of the status of teachers, increased number of provincial universities and of facilities for entering them." Gregory also drew the inevitable comparison with Germany at great length and in much detail.[114]

The British Science Guild, with Sir William Mather succeeding Haldane as president, appointed a joint committee drawn from the members of the education and technical education committees to bring in, in view of the Government's announced intentions, a comprehensive scheme of education. The committee drew up some eleven proposals, including the raising of the school leaving age to 14 years and compulsory attendance of six hours a week at continuation school up to 17 years of age. As usual, a lengthy comparison of German and English universities and higher technical schools was included.[115]

Even university education seemed to have reached a turning point. The year before the reform element at Cambridge had lost heart about the possibility of reform from within. Seeking to improve relations between the University and the colleges and the administration of funds devoted to fellowships, scholarships and exhibitions, six professors and twenty-two other members of the University circulated a memorial asking for a royal commission.[116] The next year Tillyard's critical history of the universities and university reform appeared, and the final report of the Haldane Commission on University Education in London (1909–12) was published, presenting, according to *Nature*, "for the first time a faithful sketch of what the University of London may and should be."[117]

6.

The balance struck in 1914

The activity in Britain immediately preceding the war seems in retrospect almost intended to present a summary of the British situation as contrasted with the German. A Canadian Royal Commission on Technical Education visited Britain and the Continent, making its report in 1913,[118] and in March, 1914, a report to the London County Council, providing a detailed account of the German program in technical training, compared it with that of Britain. The latter, written by J. C. Smail of the Education Department, was entitled *Trade and Technical Education in France and Germany*.[119] In presenting the report, Blair, the educational officer of the London County Council, offered a succinct summary.

> The Paris professional trade schools are training foremen, leaving these to train the workmen in the shops, whereas the German continuation schools supplement apprenticeship

and are aiming at the uplifting of every man in his fourfold aspect of member of his trade, member of his family, member of the community, and member of the State.

. . . . .

In Berlin, Munich, Leipzig and other towns the organised efforts of the State and the Municipality are reaching every boy (and in a few cases every girl) in a way that would hardly be credited in England but for the fact that experienced officers have seen it in operation. Continued education in Germany still possesses a national organisation for definite national objects.

The British method makes the best top; it also produces the worst tail, and it does not do much for the general raising of the great mass of workers. It must not be forgotten that the London evening student on the average makes 50 hours' attendance per session, while the German boy makes 240. The German boy must take three or four years continuation course; the English boy may take as much as he pleases, and 75 per cent between 14 and 17 either cannot or do not please even for one year.[120]

The Canadian Commission's report, despite its care in noting a situation presently existing "as full of promise," was damning in its reflection upon England's past. After noting that "The unsolved problem of England seems to lie with the multitudes of young people between 13 and 18 in the factory towns who are under par in physique, without the bracing stimulation of good homes and without the vision or the ambition to seek educational preparation for mature life,"[121] the report continued:

One did not find better classes or schools in Germany than in England; but the appearance of the young workers in the textile industries, for example, was immensely superior in Germany. That applied in some measure to the other factory workers in the two countries . . . The intelligence, self-control and ability, that come from the union of education and industry, are [in England] perhaps only in their fulness for the children's children.[122]

Aware as English educational authorities often were of the

critical unpreparedness of Britain to face the competition of the twentieth century, many of them had, as Haldane wrote later, "done their best among a people deficient in ideas and in interest in education."[123] But England still did not possess in 1914, as Germany had for nearly a century, "a national organisation for national objects." Opportunities for education had been provided for students who had the initiative to pursue them; that was all. As Sir William Ramsay put it, "Although the methods employed have been lamentably defective, it must be acknowledged that the democratic ideal lay at the bottom of English education . . . Stated tersely the difference in the two ideas is that between individualism and collectivism."[124]

The English, starting in the 1850's with backward and inadequate educational institutions and programs of instruction, were caught in the educational dilemma of the liberal democratic states. Concerned with universal values and the development of the individual's perception and judgment as the citizen of a self-governing state, they clung to their ideal of liberal education, while defending the individual against total absorption by his social functions. But when compared to their major competitors, and especially compared to Germany, they only inadequately met the need for specialization and the need to develop every child's capacities to the utmost in order to supply the varied demands of a modern state and society for efficient personnel. As A. N. Whitehead declared in 1916, "English education in its present form suffers from a lack of aim . . . It has not decided whether to produce amateurs or experts."[125]

The campaigns in behalf of education during the preceding quarter of a century had been waged in the interests of national efficiency in the face of national danger. For the men who most vigorously campaigned for educational reform and the advancement of science and technology and who most clearly realized the danger of conflict with Germany, whether commercial or military, were those who viewed German efficiency with the greatest admiration. Many of them, Haldane, Sadler, Schüster, Lockyer, and the foreign-born philanthropists, almost without exception, were internationalists and did not want war with Germany. But they did want to strengthen Britain in preparation for the trials of the twentieth century, and to effect this they turned inevitably to the German model.

It has often been thought that the War brought many promising new developments to an abrupt halt: the exact opposite is probably nearer the truth. In view of the leisurely approach to reform earlier, the War quickend the pace of change. When collective action was required at whatever cost, the government at last acted more decisively in the directions long urged by the reformers.

Notes

CHAPTER V

1. *Nature*, XLVII (1892–93), 201–202.

2. *Nature*, LIX (1898–99), 352, abridgement of a *Times'* report.

3. The phrase is Sadler's. On the Americans see esp. his *Secondary Education in Germany*, p. 34; J. J. Findlay's report on "Education in the United States and Canada" to Royal Commission on Secondary Education, 1895 [Cd. 7862–VI], Report of Commissioners, London, 1895. 9 vols, in 7. Cited hereafter as *Report* 1895 [– 7862]; the report of the Moseley Committee from Birmingham referred to in note 23 below. Richard Heathcote Heindel, *The American Impact on Great Britain, 1898–1914* (Philadelphia, 1940), Ch. XI, offers a random sampling of opinion.

4. F. G. Donnan, *Ludwig Mond: 1839–1909* (London, 1939), p. 6.

5. Miall, *A History of The British Chemical Industry* (London, 1931), pp. 76–77.

6. Leopold S. Amery, *My Political Life*, I, (London, 1953), pp. 184–185.

7. C. H. Firth, *Modern Languages at Oxford, 1724–1929* (Oxford and London, 1909), p. 85.

8. *Nature*, LXVII (1902–03), 300.

9. *Nature*, LI (1894–95), 217–218; LII (1895), 63–64; LIV (1896), 200–201.

10. "The problem of producing order out of chaos in London was, from the point of view of sheer organisation, the most complex that has ever presented itself in academic history." S. J. Curtis, p. 426, quoting Archer, *Secondary Education in the Nineteenth Century*.

11. *Nature*, XLVII (1892–93), 121–122; 200–201.

12. Report of the Commissioners appointed to consider the Draft Charter for the Proposed Gresham University in London, 1894, Minutes of Evidence [C.–7425], pp. 1191–1211, esp. Q. 25, 275.

13. *Nature*, XLVII (1892–93), 121.

14. Cyril Bibby, *T. H. Huxley* (London, 1959), p. 227.

15. Gresham Commission, Minutes of Evidence, pp. 692 ff. and Q. 16,844. See also the testimony of W. C. Unwin, pp. 771–779.

16. *Ibid.*, esp. testimony of W. F. R. Weldon, pp. 84–92, and of Nettleship, pp. 112–113. See also Appendix No. 8 in Appendix and Analytic Index to Minutes of Evidence, 1894 [C.–7425–1], and Foster's testimony, pp. 72–84.

17. *Ibid.*, Report, 1894 [C.–7259], p. xxi.

18. *Ibid.*, p. xxxvii. See also the account in Cardwell (London, 1929), pp. 130–131.

19. Beatrice Webb, *Our Partnership* (London, 1948), p. 95; R. B. Haldane, *An Autobiography* (London, 1929), pp. 135 ff.

20. Hansard, 4th Series, 59 (1898), 257–267; 273–278. Cf. Armytage, *Civic Universities*, p. 238.

21. Julian Amery, *Life of Joseph Chamberlain*, IV, p. 211.

22. *Ibid.*, p. 219. Cf., Armytage, *op. cit.* (note 46, Chapter III above), pp. 243–244. See also the quotation from Chamberlain's address to the University of Birmingham in 1901 on the necessity of higher education to Britain if she were to maintain "a foremost place in the rank of the nations of the world," in Sadler, *Secondary Education in Germany*, p. 160, note.

23. Amery, *op. cit.*, p. 218; *Nature*, LXII (1900), 141, 184–186; 203–206. Cf., Charles Menmuir, "The Moseley Educational Commission," *Westminster Review*, 162 (1904), 555–562, for the oft-recurring criticism of the quality of American education.

24. See Haldane, *Education and Empire*, Ch. I; and his *Universities and National Life*. See also Armytage, *op. cit.*, Ch. 11.

25. See among many others, *National Review*, XXXVI (1900–01), 178–179; XXXVIII (1901–02) 139; *Fortnightly Review*, LXXIV (1900²) 641.

26. Lord Avebury, "The Future of Europe," *Nineteenth Century*, LIX (1906¹), 416–428.

27. *Nature*, LXIV (1901), 221, reporting an address at the Imperial Institute.

28. Among many, see *Nature*, LXIV (1901), 500; LIX (1898–99), 306–307.

29. *Nature*, LX (1899), 551–554.

30. London, 1901. First delivered as a lecture in 1900.

31. *Nature*, LXIII (1900–01), Supplement for March 21, pp. iii–iv.

32. *Ibid.*, pp. v–vi.

33. *The Nineteenth Century*, XLIX (1901¹), 57–63.

34. *Nature*, LXV (1901–02), 585.

35. *Ibid.*, 69–70.
36. *The Nineteenth Century*, XLIX (1901[1]), 1028–1037.
37. *Ibid.*, 348–363.
38. *Nature*, LXIV (1901), 503–509.
39. *Nature*, LXV (1901–02), 138–139.
40. Report, 1895 [C.–7862], *passim.* See also, H. E. Roscoe, "The Secondary Education Movement," *Nature*, XLIX (1893–94), 203–204; R. A. Gregory, "The Advance of Technical Education," *Nature*, LI (1894–95), 380. Cf., Curtis, *op. cit.*, p. 180; also, Amery, *op. cit.*, p. 492.
41. See Lynda Grier, *Achievement in Education, The Work of Michael Ernest Sadler* (London, 1952), Ch. II.
42. Report, *op. cit.*, p. 70.
43. Report, *op. cit.*, I, p. 86. See also the account in Curtis, *op. cit.*, pp. 308–310.
44. *Nature*, LXIV (1901), 564.
45. Bernard M. Allen, *Sir Robert Morant* (London, 1934), 134 ff. Cf., Lynda Grier, *op. cit.*, esp. pp. 80–91; Amery, *op. cit.*, IV, pp. 478–508; Curtis, *op. cit.*, pp. 313–321.
46. *Nature*, LXV (1901–02), 562. See the debate in the *The Nineteenth Century*, LI (1902[1]), esp. 602–624.
47. Curtis, *op. cit.*, p. 320. Halévy, *Epilogue*, Vol. I, p. 205, noted that "England had seen the necessity of copying the Continental, the Prussian example . . ."
48. M. E. Sadler, *Secondary Education in Germany*, quoted on p. 40.
49. *Ibid.*, p. 172, Appendix I.
50. Technical Education Board of the London County Council Report of the Special Sub-Committee on the Application of Science to Industry, (London, 1902), p. 3.
51. *Ibid.*, p. 4.
52. *Ibid.*, p. 5. See also Cardwell, *op. cit.*, pp. 149–150.
53. See Thomas Lloyd Humberstone, *University Reform in London* (London, 1926), Appendix II, p. 174.
54. *Ibid.*, pp. 167–170, where Rosebery's letter is reproduced. See also *Nature*, LXVIII (1903), 203–204.
55. *Nature*, LXXII (1905), 69–70, 233–235, 251; and LXXXI (1909), 83-84. See also Haldane, *op. cit.*, pp. 154–155; Final Report, Board of Education Department Committee on the Royal College of Science, etc., 1906 [Cd. 2872]. In addition to Haldane, the Committee included Edward Carbutt, Philip Magnus, Arthur Rücker, Sidney Webb, Julius Wernher, and William H. White.
56. *Nature*, LXXIII (1905–06), 345.
57. *Nature*, LXVIII (1903), 438–447. The address was reprinted by Lockyer, *Education and National Progress* (London, 1906), pp. 172–215.

58. *Nature*, LXX (1904), 271–72; see also Lockyer, *op. cit.*, pp. 216–221.

59. *Nature*, LXX, 275.

60. *Nature*, LXXIII (1905–06), 10–13.

61. *Nature*, LXXXVII (1911), 118.

61a. *Nature*, LXXIII (1905–06), 10–12.

62. *Nature*, LXXV (1906–07), 37–38.

63. All quotations from *Nature*, LXXVII (1907–08), 153–154.

64. See the figures in Cardwell, p. 155, where a comparison with the Prussian figures is also given.

65. Report of the British Association for the Advancement of Science, Belfast, 1902 (London, 1903), 3–50. The role that the Royal Institution played in scientific instruction has been greatly exaggerated. It provided a meager living, roughly the equivalent of Oxford or Cambridge fellowships, to a few distinguished scientific researchers.

66. *Nature*, LXVI (1902), 465–67.

67. *Ibid.*, 211–214.

68. *Nature*, LXXI (1904–05), 108.

69. *Nature*, LV (1896–97), 612–613. See also Mallet, III, pp. 352–353, 482; J. H. Clapham, *An Economic History of Modern Britain* (Cambridge, 1926–38), III, pp. 76 ff.

70. See Sir J. J. Thomson, *Recollections and Reflections* (London, 1936), esp. pp. 136–138. *Nature*, LII (1895), 298.

71. Percy Gardner, *Oxford at the Cross Roads* (London, 1903), p. 57; see also Farnell, *op. cit.* (note 28, Chapter II above), p. 272.

72. See C. A. Firth, *Inaugural Address* (Oxford, 1904), esp. p. 19; and his *The School of English Language and Literature*, pp. 31–47; and *Modern Languages at Oxford*, pp. 74 ff.

73. See F. S. C. Schiller, "Examination v. Research," *Nature*, LXXVII (1907–08), 322–324.

74. *Nature*, LXXV (1907), 404.

75. Among the signers were Henry Balfour, T. K. Cheyne, R. B. Clifton, S. R. Driver, Robinson Ellis, Arthur J. Evans, C. H. Firth, Percy Gardner, R. W. Macan, A. S. Napier, W. Odling, H. F. Pelham, E. B. Poulton, H. Sidgwick, John Rhys, W. Sanday, A. H. Sayce, Henry Sweet, E. B. Tylor, Sydney Vines, W. F. R. Weldon, and Joseph Wright. *Nature*, LXXII (1905), 231.

76. *Nature*, LXXVI (1907), 35–37.

77. *Nature*, LXXV (1906–07), 337–339. Hansard, 4th Series (1907), 178, 1526–1539.

78. See Farnell, *op. cit.* (note 28, Chapter II above), p. 282. Farnell dates the incident in 1913, but he appears to have been mistaken in this.

79. *Nature*, LXXXVIII (1911–12), 478. See Congress of the Universities of the Empire, *Report of Proceedings*, ed. Alan Hill (London, 1912). Parkin had been working to establish such an organization

since the Allied Colonial Universities Conference in 1903, of which he had been the moving spirit. See *Nature*, LXVIII (1903), 251.

80. See his *Principles and Methods of University Reform* (London, 1909), pp. 307–323, Tillyard, *op. cit.* (note 32, Chapter III above), Chs. X, XI; Mallet, pp. 477–480.

81. See the detailed account by Schüster, "International Science," an address to the Royal Society, *Nature*, LXXIV (1906), 233–237, 256–259. Cf. Lyons, p. 293; G. C. Simpson, "Sir Arthur Schüster," *Obituary Notices of Fellows of The Royal Society*, I (London, 1932–35), pp. 409–423.

82. *Nature*, LXV (1901–02), 289–291.

83. See A. V. Dicey, "A Chartered Academy," *The Nineteenth Century*, LI (1902[1]), 493–505. In due course Dicey became a member.

84. *Nature*, LXVII (1902–03), 104.

85. A. F. Pollard, *The Claims of Historical Research in London*, a pamphlet (London, 1920), p. 3.

86. *Nature*, LXXVII (1907–08), 362.

87. *Nature*, LXXIX (1908–09), 493.

88. *Nature*, LXXXII (1909–10), 326.

89. *Ibid.*, 471–475.

90. *Nature*, LXXXVI (1911), 128.

91. *Nature*, LXXXVII (1911), 93.

92. Report of Advisory Committee on University Grants, Board of Education, 1912–1913 [Cd. 6140], p. 4.

93. See the statements by E. H. Starling in Royal Commission on the University of London, Fifth Report, 1912 [Cd. 6311], pp. 194–204; and by Sir Henry Head, pp. 140–142.

94. Stephen Paget, *Memoirs and Letters of Sir James Paget* (London, 1901), p. 52.

95. See Charles Newman, *The Evolution of Medical Education in The Nineteenth Century* (London, 1957), p. 305.

96. See Sir Humphrey Davy Rolleston, *The Cambridge Medical School* (Cambridge, 1932).

97. See *Obituary Notices of the Fellows of The Royal Society* I, (1932–35) and "Bruce, Sir David," *D. N. B.*

98. *Ibid.*, pp. 26–30.

99. Studied with Stricker in Vienna.

100. *Obituary Notices of The Fellows of The Royal Society* II (1936–38), pp. 493–499.

101. *Ibid.*, I, pp. 108–113.

102. *Ibid.*, II, pp. 493–499.

103. Cuthbert Dukes, *Lord Lister (1827–1912)* (London, 1924), pp. 158–159.

104. *Ibid.*, pp. 157–158.

105. See Harvey Cushing, *The Life of William Osler* (Oxford, 1925), I p. 650f.

106. *Ibid.*, II, pp. 190, 244.

107. Abraham Flexner, *I Remember* (New York, 1940), p. 138.

108. See Royal Commission on University Education in London, Third Report, Minutes of Evidence, 1911, [Cd. 5911] for the testimony of Flexner, Max Müller, and Osler.

109. Appendix to Fifth Report, Minutes of Evidence, 1912 [Cd. 6312], Q. 14,668, 14,681.

110. Abraham Flexner, *Medical Education in Europe* (New York, 1912), pp. 255 ff.

111. *Ibid.*, pp. vii, viii.

112. *Nature*, XCI (1913), 215. See also "The Vision of a London University," *The Nation*, 13 (1913).

113. *Nature*, XC (1912–13), 546–547. See also Haldane's remarks, 13 October 1913 at Sheffield: "The main features of the Board of Education's scheme are a recognition of the great strides being made in university education by the United States and Germany." *Nature*, XCII (1913–14), 270–271.

114. "National Aspects of Education," *Nature*, XCI (1913), 171–174.

115. "The British Science Guild," *Ibid.*, 331–332.

116. *Nature*, LXXXIX (1912), 280.

117. *Nature*, XCI (1913), 215.

118. Report of the Royal Commission on Industrial Training and Technical Education, vol. I, Part III (Ottawa, 1913).

119. London County Council, Education Dept. Trade and Technical Education in France and Germany. Report by Education Officer Submitting a Report by Mr. J. C. Smail, Organiser of Trade Schools for Boys, on Technical Education in France and Germany, London, 1914.

120. R. Blair in foreword, to work cited in note 119 (no pagination).

121. Report of The Royal Commission . . . (see note 118 above), Part III, Vol. I, p. 445.

122. *Ibid.*, p. 446.

123. In R. B. Haldane's "National Education" in William Harbutt Dawson, ed., *After-War Problems* (New York, 1917), p. 86.

124. Quoted in William Tilden, *op. cit.*, p. 198. See also Morris Travers, *A Life of William Ramsay* (London, 1956).

125. In his presidential address to the Mathematical Association of England, reprinted in *The Aims of Education* (1929). Quotation cited from 1955 reprint, p. 25.

Chapter VI

The Response to World War I

For a quarter of a century before 1914 W. H. Dawson was indefatigable in keeping his countrymen informed on the institutional and industrial development of Germany. Introducing a collection of essays on *After-War Problems* in 1917, he remarked that those who had warned of the activities of other countries, and especially of Germany, had "preached in season and out of season their sermons on the prosy texts of Order, Authority, Discipline, Organization, Patriotism, the greater merging of the one in the all." He lamented that for the most part their warnings had gone unheeded.[1]

A reason for this neglect was to be found in the flourishing condition of the British economy in the decade before the war. For if the decline in real wages is ignored, Britain was prosperous. Despite all the uneasiness about industry expressed by the tariff reformers, scientists, educators, and journalists, and despite the more rapid growth-rate of the German and American industries, until the War, Britain's position as the leading industrial state was on the whole maintained. London remained the banking center of the world; never had more British capital gone abroad for investment. Britain's merchant fleet far surpassed any other in tonnage; never had British shipyards produced and exported more merchant shipping than in the early years of the twentieth century. Industrial production and foreign commerce continued to increase, reaching figures well above the highest levels attained in the nineteenth century; never had Britain produced and exported more coal, more textiles, nor had British ships carried more goods both for export and import. Although British industries could not before the war have alone maintained a favorable trade balance, such a balance was maintained by receipts from foreign investments, shipping, and the financing and insuring of trade. It was possible for Englishmen to believe then, as most economic historians from Alfred Marshall in 1921 to William Ashworth in 1960 have since, that in spite of all criticism the British economy was with minor reservations still sound.[2]

Nevertheless, as early as 1900 certain of the more important British industries exhibited irrefutable evidence of an inability to meet foreign competition. In such basic products as pig-iron and steel, and even in coal and textiles, the percentage of Britain's share in world production was falling. In steel, Britain fell to third in total output, being surpassed by both the United States and Germany.[3] Neither were these industries, despite their prosperity, maintaining peak efficiency in production relative to their chief competitors. But the conventional industries of the industrial revolution were not the center of weakness in Britain's industrial life. More important was the British failure to develop proportionately with her greatest rivals the new technological industries: chemicals, electricity, metallurgy and optics.[4] Britain's weakness lay in the industries most closely associated with scientific technology, where advanced education and research, planning and professional direction were required. And these industries were not only fundamental for the growth of the old industries, they were also increasingly the sources for the growth or expansion of any twentieth-century advanced industrial economy.[5]

Looking at British industry as a whole in the pre-war years, one is confronted with the picture of an old-established, insular, industrial economy, almost accidentally predominant in world markets. Nowhere was the chaos of British institutional life more evident. Innumerable independent, privately-owned, large and small companies provided a great diversity of products usually in small lots, and their strength lay in quality rather than in mass production. The manufacturers were parochial in outlook. Their sales, especially foreign, were made through merchant distribution. Though incorporated in limited companies, their shares were often very closely held, frequently by a single family, and their financing was usually undertaken by local bankers. Owners and managers had generally little formal education, rarely beyond secondary school and often limited to grammar school. They operated by rule-of-thumb or the well-known "practical experience." Indifferent to, when not oblivious of, advances made in similar industries elsewhere, they tended to be suspicious of each other, secretive, often complacent and arrogant, and they rarely hired men professionally trained either in commerce or technology, such men being in any case hard to find. As a result of inadequate reinvestment in plant, obsolescence was not unusual when compared with the plants of their overseas competitors. Despite a flurry of consolidations into large organizations among a few industries around the turn of the century, British industries remained largely unconsolidated nationally. A host of loosely organized trade associations attempted to deal with labor and to control prices, but they were weak and limited to specific industries.[6]

This was the consequence of the open, competitive society which encouraged and protected individual, private enterprise, and most Englishmen regarded such industrial chaos with unadulterated pride. Few foresaw that nearly every one of the cultural characteristics, faithfully mirrored in this industrial picture, which had served Britain so well in the nineteenth century was to become disadvantageous in the highly nationalistic, competitive society of the twentieth. The localism of business, the individualism which discouraged cooperation other than through loose associations, the faith in the beneficence of free and open competition and the "natural" adjustment of prices by the market, to the benefit of the consumer, the distrust of governmental "interference", and the distrust of the expert and of theoretical knowledge in general had all contributed to the strength of British industry for over a century, but in the new international competition all of these were to appear as weaknesses. Against them the reformers, whether scientists, scholars, statesmen, or industrialists, protested, as it was these very beliefs and practices which were proved inadequate by the examples of Germany and the United States.

Whatever else may be said of British industry in 1914, it was in almost every way unfitted to service a modern, technological war. To judge an economy by its potential efficiency in war would have seemed irrational to orthodox liberal economists. But to do so was certainly reasonable in the case of a great power state with an empire to rule and to protect. War was an accepted recourse of action for independent national states, as the very existence of the British fleet and the British army in numerous outposts, including India, acknowledged, even had Britain not recently engaged in war. Tested by war, the British economy was not only not self-sufficient; in the twentieth century it could not support a great power. And if Britain could not be a great power, she might not be able to survive as an independent power and certainly not as an enormously wealthy state with a far-flung empire. That was what twentieth century imperialists, such as Chamberlain, Garvin, Mackinder, Amery, Milner, and the members of the Compatriots Club in general, understood. Others had to learn by the test of war that the only European combatant with the economic potentials of a great power in 1914 was Germany.

War and the fear of war are probably the strongest promoters of acculturation in the modern world. Certain it is that no sooner was war declared than the British proceeded to do what the reformers had for so long been urging in admiration and fear of Germany. And what was done, though far too little, was in line with the German-influenced proposals for "order, authority, discipline, and organization." The Government acted because a national emergency created an acceptance of collective devices, and if much of the collectivism of the war years was to be rapidly dispensed with immediately the war was concluded, the work had been done; the experience of cooperation rather than competition had been enjoyed; new organizations had been founded, and new ideas planted. The seeds of a collectivist business world, sown in the cultivated soil of leadership responsibility during the war, would in due time bear fruit.

Economic historians who have dismissed the War of 1914 as an unpleasant interlude, an aberration in the normal development of the British economy, who have seen it only as a great disruptive agency, have overlooked its true significance. Contemporaries knew better. "The war, in the Prime Minister's phrase . . . has been as 'a star-shell illuminating the dark places in our national life.' It has 'revealed with pitiless accuracy the defects in our industrial equipment.' "[7]

The War compelled Britain's industrial leaders at last to look at their economy from a national political standpoint in an era of hard international competition and to compare it with their enemy's. At once they saw that Germany, aggressive industrially and commercially, had been with strong state support and supervision, startlingly and dangerously successful. They were led to conclude that to permit their own economy to operate without direction, supervision, or control might well lead to political disaster in a world where the economies of other great states were politically oriented.

Looked at in this new light, English industry exhibited glaring weaknesses. First, there was a shortage of many raw materials and technological industries without which no industrialized state could effectively defend itself in modern war: what came to be known as "key" materials and industries. Control or development of many of these was wholly inadequate in Britain in 1914. A second weakness, as quickly spotted, was the inadequacy of scientific research in industry. This inadequacy pointed in turn directly to the failure of English education to fulfill the reformers' "second purpose" of education: to fit men for the work necessary to the state. A third weakness was the multiplicity of small, independent, competing units in nearly every industry. Even when efficient, their very size denied them the resources to sustain research for expansion and to reduce the costs of production and distribution.

Under the impact of war, many British industrialists discovered, as so many scientists, journalists, and statesmen had long insisted, that where Germany excelled Britain was weak: in scientific education, in technological research, and in industrial organization. And as the statesmen had followed the German model in social legislation, the industrialists turned also to the example of Germany. Although they might more easily have studied American practices, and to some extent did so, it was their enemy they especially sought to copy.

1.

Government-sponsored research and educational reform

If it be recalled that, despite the terrible loss of men in the War, damage to physical plant was negligible apart from heavy wear, it might appear extraordinary that a Ministry of Reconstruction would be appointed. It was not merely a social conscience at work to make "a land fit for heroes to live in," though that played a part. Rather it was the recognition that a reorganization of British life, and particularly a reconstruction of its industrial life, was required in the interest of national efficiency, as the reformers had for long been insisting. The revelations occasioned by the War stimulated action as nothing else would have done, bringing home to many industrialists and others what had been evident before only to a few.

Under the pressure of a great emergency, the Government did what the Devonshire Commission and so many others had recommended. In the spring of 1915 an Order in Council established a Committee of the Privy Council for Scientific and Industrial Research upon which, in addition to the Ministers of the Exchequer, the Board of Trade, and the Board of Education, were A. H. D. Acland and R. B. Haldane. This Committee in turn appointed an Advisory Council, to become in 1916–17 a Department of Scientific and Industrial Research "to organise research on a national scale," and allotted it £50,000 the first year to expend on research projects. Among the first members were W. S. McCormick of the University Grants Committee; the physicist, Lord Rayleigh; the chemist, Raphael Meldola, succeeded upon his death by J. F. Thorpe; B. Hopkinson, shortly replaced by C. A. Parsons, electrical engineer; and Richard Threlfall, the Director of the National Physical Laboratory.[8]

Such a Council was certain to understand the importance of "basic science," but they found that the Universities had been so stripped of men that the encouragement of original scientific research had to be left to the post-war years. Their immediate attention was therefore directed to the application of science to industry. Here the division of industries into many small independent units hampered them. Easiest to begin with were the engineering trades where the professional societies had already made a start in promoting research. They found the chemical trades, however, "so divided and individual in outlook that the various professional societies have had neither the influence nor the means necessary to enable them to take any large share in promoting research."[9] The textile trades had made even less progress;

they were "content . . . to leave science to the dyers and the dye-stuff manufacturers . . . without much care . . . as to their nation-ality." The same was true of the paper manufacturers and a long list of others.[10]

The smallness of many undertakings prevented the introduction of industrial research even when the industrialists were interested in doing so. Banks would not finance research and the managers "whose training and experience have been confined to their own industry . . . are therefore apt to resist proposals for improve-ment."[11] One needs hardly to be told that the Council had Ger-many in mind when observing that: "Organisation can only be fought by counter organisation, and so long as the Englishman treats his business house as his business castle . . . with his hand against the hand of every other baron in his trade and no personal interest in the foreign politics of his industry as a whole, it will be . . . impossible for the State to save him."[12] The English indus-trialists might reasonably have inquired of the Council what Eng-lish economists, other than those associated with the Compatriots' Club, had ever asked him to look at his industry "as a whole", let alone take a personal interest in its foreign politics.

The Council proceeded to award research grants to individual laboratories and to encourage members of industries and associa-tions connected with them to form associations for joint research undertakings. Four such associations had been formed by 1918 and many more were to follow. They attempted also to establish research directories and in general to give national organization and direction to scientific industrial research. The National Phys-ical Laboratory was turned over to them and their responsibilities continued to be enlarged.

The implications of the work being done by this government council did not escape a commentator in *Nature* where one might have expected only enthusiastic approval. He observed that in Germany the various technological associations had formed a "German Union of Technical Scientific Societies" for the same purposes, but in Germany it was these societies and industries which assumed the responsibility rather than the government. In England, "we . . . who have hitherto been proud of our individ-ualistic principles, which have ever formed the basis of Britain's industrial greatness, are content to sink our individualism and to ask a Government Department to solve our industrial problems for us."[13] True as the comment was, the writer overlooked the failure of English education to provide for the educational needs in science, the failure of English industrialists to give proper value to scientific research in their industries, and perhaps of the technical associations to establish close relations with the industries. The former pride in individualism had brought the State into a position of grave danger and such collectivism as the Council represented was a consequence. The Government acted because of the failure of individuals, industries, and technical societies to meet their national responsibilities.

While whole industries needed to be persuaded of the importance of research laboratories on the pattern of the American and German, prerequisite to the encouragement of research was the need for scientific education. Many more students were needed in more universities with better paid professors and better paid openings in industry. There were needed, too, special research institutes associated with the universities but also closely allied with industries.[14] The Council concluded its Report for 1916–17 with a statement almost echoing the words of Bulwer-Lytton a century before.

> Our people have no reason to fear or envy the scientific pioneers of other races. They have had, and will probably continue to have, their full share of the outstanding minds . . . but as time goes on the sphere of the solitary worker tends to become relatively, if not absolutely, smaller. Effective research, particularly in its industrial applications, calls increasingly for the support and impetus that come from the systematised delving of a corps of sappers working intelligently, but under orders. We have not yet learned how to make the most of mediocre ability—particularly in things of the mind—yet without the scientific rank and file it will be as impossible to staff the industrial research laboratories which are coming, as to fight a European war with seven divisions.[15]

A similar statement was repeated in their subsequent reports, care being taken to point out that the best the Council itself could do toward this end would inevitably be but partial and insufficient. "The responsibility for recruiting the army of men and women we need must lie upon the Education Authorities of the country."[16]

Stimulated by the Council and by the scientific societies, the educational ferment seemed at last to penetrate into all sections of the community. Nearly all the industrial committees agreed in principle with the recommendations made by the Committee on the Iron and Steel Trades. Dissatisfied with the lack of systematic technical instruction on a scale commensurate with the needs of the industry, they found that the whole educational system suffered from the "defect of discontinuity," and they set forth in outline a specific program of reform. The limit of the school-leaving age should be raised from 14 to 16 years. Apprenticeship might begin, however, at 14 under an indenture contract of seven years' service, but technical education should be continued as "a matter of routine" to 18 years, with an allowance of six hours a week during the day, preferably in the morning, with six hours of homework or reading in addition. Though the studies were to be predominantly scientific, the literary side was not to be neglected. After 18 years of age, higher or university education should begin for all who gave promise of benefiting by it. For this purpose a technical institute of university level should be founded in every large industrial center with which local industries should be in intimate cooperation.[17] It was the old demand for an educational ladder to be allied with industrial participation.

By the time these reports were published, H. A. L. Fisher, the first professional educator to serve as President of the Board of Education, was ready with an Education Bill embodying some of these proposals. The school-leaving age was raised to 14 with permission for local authorities to raise it to 15. Compulsory day continuation schools were to be founded for those not otherwise in school up to 16 years of age and in seven years this was to be raised to 18. Provisions were made for medical inspection, nursery schools, and other services, the extent, however, being left to the discretion of the local authorities. Fees were abolished in the elementary schools but not in the secondary schools, though many scholarships were to be made available. The Education Act of 1918 marked an advance over all previous legislation for education but it left much to voluntary local initiative. No sooner had the War ended than even some of the compulsory features including the raising of the school-leaving age, were honored only in the breach; many of the continuation schools were not provided, and the whole was emasculated in varying degrees in the harsh economic climate of the twenties.

Other committees studied the position of the modern languages and of science in education. The Committee on Modern Languages found that in twenty-two separate institutions of university rank "there were, all told, seventy persons to teach French and everything that pertains to France."[18] Cambridge, Bristol, and the four Scottish Universities had no professorship of French; the same universities, omitting Cambridge, had no professorship of German. "There was not a single professorship of Italian, only two of Spanish, one of these created during the war, and one of Russian."[19] The Committee accused the general public and business men of indifference and apathy,[20] a charge to be levelled against England generally by the Royal Commission on Oxford and Cambridge Universities in 1922.[21] While a few business firms encouraged their employees to learn foreign languages, and a good many sent their clerks abroad, too many "seemed to prefer the easiest course, that of grumbling at British education, and employing the cheap labour of German clerks and travellers."[22] Persuaded that "a majority of the pupils did not acquire through the classics any satisfying education," they urged that "neither Greek nor Latin be compulsory for an Arts degree in any of our Universities."[23]

Unlike most of the committees at this time, this committee wished to be rid of one German-inherited influence. They found the teaching which centered around philology, "the study of words as words and of language for its own sake," inadequate. Literature should not "fail to develop imaginative sympathy" as a means of acquiring knowledge of a foreign people.[24]

At Cambridge a reform in modern studies was in progress with the founding of a Tripos in English in 1917. Partly a reaction against the study of literature as philology, it was in part a patriotic interest in opposing the German emphasis on pre-Chaucerian studies. The movement stemmed also from E. B. Moore's revolt

against idealism, while owing perhaps as much to the development
of anthropology and to the shift which occurred in classical studies
with the development of archaeology, an interest in culture in the
old German idealist and new anthropological sense of the word.
Contributing to the movement were such men as J. Churton
Collins, no scholar in the German sense, and A. W. Ward, long a
teacher of the history of English Literature at the University of
London; and the example' of the provincial universities and of
Oxford, where an English Honours School was gradually assuming form before 1914 under Walter Raleigh.[25]

Studying the place of the sciences in education was a distinguished committee under the chairmanship of J. J. Thomson with
Henry Head, E. H. Starling, and Michael Sadler among its members. Impressed with the need for "a great increase in the supply
of trained scientific workers of all grades," they argued for the
inclusion of science at all educational levels, specifying in detail
the time and subjects to be studied from the elementary school
through the university. In urging that the First School Examination be accepted as entrance qualification both to medical schools
and universities, they followed the recommendations of the Haldane
Commission and the practice of the Germans. They stressed the
need for Oxford and Cambridge to provide suitable science courses
for candidates not aiming at an honors degree in the subject. For
all science degrees research should be a requirement, and they
recommended the abolition of Greek as compulsory in responsions
at Oxford and the Previous Examination at Cambridge.[26]

The report of this committee was followed up by R. A. Gregory
in a long article in *Nature*. Assuming Lockyer's old mantle, in the
now established fashion he drew a detailed comparison of the
German, American, and English universities. The failure of private
philanthropy in England compared with the United States was
again documented: the limited number of English university students, relative to the population, when compared with either Germany or America, and the great inferiority in the number of science students. British universities were shown to be much more
heavily dependent upon student fees than either of the other two.
In Germany, the single University of Berlin "receives annually
from State funds a grant nearly equal to the total annual Parlia-

mentary grants to the universities and colleges of England and Wales." In the United States, government grants were even greater; there "nine universities . . . have individual incomes exceeding the total amount granted by Parliament to universities and institutions of like standard in the United Kingdom."[27] However, despite the efforts of the committees and many others, action to reform the universities was to await the Royal Commission on Oxford and Cambridge in 1920 and another commission on London University in 1926.

Furtherance of medical research had already proceeded before the War as a result of the National Insurance Act. Under that Act a Medical Research Committee had established its own Central Research Department. At the same time it supported research in various laboratories, hospitals, medical schools, and universities throughout the country. Reporting in 1916–17 the Committee significantly noted that "In the early stages of the war, while our deficiencies due to our former failures to encourage or to apply the work of science were widely deplored, it was very common nevertheless to hear that research should be laid aside 'till the war is over'. Bitter need in every direction of the contest, and not least upon the medical side, has shown how vital the spirit of inquiry is to success in this prolonged competition of national efficiencies."[28]

But a start in the reform of medical education was also to be made. Sir George Newman, chief medical officer to the Board of Education, published in 1918 *Some Notes on Medical Education in England*. A new situation faced the medical profession. Under the National Insurance Act of 1911, 14 million persons in England had become eligible for medical benefits, leading to a greatly increased demand for physicians and an expansion of clinical and hospital services. Noting that already over 15 thousand physicians were in the pay of the State on a whole or part-time basis and many others served the State in a variety of matters, Newman concluded that "medicine has become a quasi-public profession." At the same time the medical schools were finding the proprietary system unprofitable. Between 1908 and 1914, out of the 22 medical schools in England and Wales, 18 had applied for and begun to receive grants from the Board of Education. He concluded that in order to meet the needs of the physician and the State, medical education had to be reformed. Only one sort of education was any longer adequate and "that is a university education in medicine. And the foundation of such an education is science."[29]

Recapitulating the criticisms of medical education made before the Haldane Commission, he repeated that Commission's recommendations. Students should be prepared in the basic sciences before entering medical school. The school should be under university supervision with paid teachers who should also be researchers. Close association between laboratories and hospital clinics was necessary; the laboratory and the demonstration lecture should replace the "systematic" lecture. Clinical, medical, and surgical units should be established in the hospitals under the direction of the university professors. Retained should be "the English system of 'apprenticeship' in the form of clerking, dressing and hospital appointments by which every student gains free and continual access to the patients both in the receiving room and at the bedside."[30]

The next year Newman was able to inform Dr. Harvey Cushing of Yale University that his pamphlet had "increased interest on the part of the Government in Medical Education and a very substantial increase of their grants-in-aid. We hope very shortly to be starting some first rate Clinical Units . . . and I expect the Government will find half to three-quarters of the expenditure incurred."[31] Because of the demonstrated importance of medicine to the State, the Treasury approved of the recommendation of the Haldane Commission, as re-enforced by Newman, and undertook to subsidize the plan for medical, surgical and clinical units under the control of university professors by an annual subsidy. By 1926 six of the medical schools had organized such units under the auspices of the University of London.[32]

By the conclusion of the War, the general pattern of government assistance in the realm of technical and university education, including scientific research, had all unknowingly been set. The University Grants Committee, transferred to the Treasury, would continue to increase its aid, including in 1919 for the first time the Universities of Oxford and Cambridge. The Medical Research Council would support the National Institute for Medical Research at Hampstead plus a variety of research projects in hospitals and universities. The Department of Scientific and Industrial Research would support various special projects in innumerable laboratories, industrial or educational. That was the pattern and despite the role of the State, it retained peculiarly individualistic features. The British preferred to give scholarships to deserving individuals rather than to make education free; they preferred to approve individual research projects rather than to provide the great laboratories for all comers.

Both a fear of wasting money on unproven individuals—and this had a reasonable basis after 1921—and a preference for individual treatment determined the pattern. As Abraham Flexner was to observe, however, these Government-sponsored committees and councils for research "seemed to say: 'We lack developed universities. While we are waiting for them or in preparation for them, let us train this or that promising man, let us get this or that thing done,' It is all very well but it does not answer."[33] In part unwilling, and in part unable to take the plunge of reconstructing their educational system, the English had compromised again. Between accepting the necessity of constructing a technologically-oriented society with all the centralized planning, direction, and sacrifice of individualism that entailed, and retaining their traditional ways with ad hoc modifications necessitated by an emergency, they did not so much choose as accept the latter as satisfactory. If it did not answer, it was because the emergency did not pass away.

Sadler's contrast between England and German educational procedures in the nineteenth century was equally appropriate to the period in England in which he wrote (1915).

> England hesitated between two opposing theories, the theory of State control and the theory of group autonomy under the general supervision of the State. Germany came to a decisive conclusion on this fundamental question of procedure. Great Britain (and particularly England) remained divided in conviction about it, and therefore irresolute in policy. Germany standardised her education upon a system. Britain, distrustful of State control, compromised.[34]

It was the old dilemma of a free, open society with representative government, strongly believing in the individual's right to choice of ends and the distribution of power among many subsidiary corporations and autonomous local groups on the one hand, and on the other a paternalist, dynastic society committed to direction, supervision, and control from the center. The British (and particularly English) solution in education and research, arrived at, as on previous occasions, almost accidentally, reflected (as did the Whitley councils devised in this period) the last rays of the effort of a social liberalism to find a *via media* between the collectivisms of the right and left without commitment and without fundamental change. Britain was still a class-structured society; to break the barriers between the classes and the masses, even in education, was impossible. Nor, it should be added, did the German influence do anything to encourage that. The exceptional lad from the masses could be taken care of through the paternalism of scholarships. Faced by the great totalitarian dictatorships of the Soviet Union and the Third Reich, in which state control and direction reached new and formerly undreamt of dimensions, the British had to make do with these makeshifts for better or worse for a quarter of a century.

Notes

CHAPTER VI

1. W. H. Dawson, ed., *After War Problems* (London, 1917), p. 9.
2. Alfred Marshall, *Industry and Trade* (London, 1919), pp. 95–99, 627–650; and Clapham, *op. cit.* (note 69, Chapter V above), III, p. 71, were reluctant to believe British industry was in trouble before 1914. More recent writers are beginning to concede this, though with apologetic reservations. See William Ashworth, *An Economic History of England, 1870–1939* (London, 1961), pp. 104–105, 151–153, 257–261, 301; Sidney Pollard, *The Development of the British Economy, 1914–1950* (London, 1962), pp. 3–10; S. B. Saul, *Studies in British Overseas Trade, 1870–1914* (London, 1960), pp. 37–42.
3. Pollard, *op. cit.*, p. 5.
4. Marshall, *op. cit.*, p. 133; Clapham, *op. cit.*, pp. 128–138; Pollard, *op. cit.*, pp. 6–9.
5. Ashworth, *op. cit.*, p. 107.

6. Marshall, *op. cit.*, p. 132.

7. Quoted in *Nature*, CII (1918–19), 507. Ashworth, *op. cit.*, p. 301, is particularly clear on this.

8. Report of the Committee of the Privy Council for Scientific and Industrial Research, 1916 [Cd. 8336], p. 11, and Appendices I, and II. The Report will hereafter be cited as D.S.I.R.

9. *Ibid.*, p. 26.

10. *Ibid.*, p. 27.

11. *Ibid.*, p. 26.

12. *Ibid.*, p. 27.

13. *Nature*, CI (1918), 206–207.

14. D.S.I.R., 1916, pp. 33–35.

15. *Ibid.*, pp. 40–41.

16. D.S.I.R., 1917–18 [Cd. 9144], p. 11.

17. Iron and Steel report, pp. 39–41.

18. See Great Britain Board of Education, *Modern Studies*, Report of the Committee on the Position of Modern Languages in the Educational System of Great Britain (London, 1918), p. 24.

19. *Ibid.*, p. 141.

20. *Ibid.*, pp. 29, 53.

21. [Cd. 1588].

22. *Modern Studies, op. cit.*, p. 25.

23. *Ibid.*, pp. 19, 217.

24. *Ibid.*, pp. 49–50.

25. See Tillyard, *The Muse Unchained*, pp. 19–63.

26. Report of the Committee on the Position of Natural Science in Education, 1918 [Cd. 9011]. See also the review in *Nature*, CI (1918), 135–136.

27. *Nature*, CI (1918), 473–477.

28. Medical Research Committee, Third Annual Report, 1916–17 [Cd. 8825], p. 8.

29. Board of Education, 1918 [Cd. 9124], p. 18.

30. *Ibid.*, esp. pp. 77–78; quotation from p. 26.

31. From a letter dated 1 April, 1919 in Dr. Cushing's copy of Newman's little book in the Medical Library of Yale University.

32. Report of the Departmental Committee on the University of London, 1926 [Cd. 2612], p. 13. See also Sir D'Arcy Power, *Short History of St. Bartholomew's Hospital* (London, 1923) pp. 94–96.

33. Abraham Flexner, *Universities, American, English, German* (New York, 1930) p. 298. His criticisms throughout support the analysis made here.

34. Quoted in *Nature* XCV (1915), 340 from *German Culture: the Contributions of the Germans to Knowledge, Literature, Art, and Life*, ed. W. P. Paterson (London, 1915).

Appendix I

Principal Publications of
George Haines IV

1. "Trends in Quakerism: 1900–1940,"
   Pennsylvania Magazine of History & Biography, January, 1942, 84–93.
2. "Forms of Imaginative Prose: 1900–1940,"
   Southern Review, VII, #4 (Spring, 1942), 755–775.
3. "Art Forms and Science Concepts,"
   Journal of Philosophy, Vol. XL #18 (Sept. 2, 1943), 482–491.
4. "Global War and the Study of History,"
   Social Forces, Vol. 22, No. 2 (Dec., 1943), 142–149.
5. With John Herman Randall, Jr.,
   "Controlling Assumptions in the Practice of American Historians,"
   Theory and Practice in Historical Study, Social Science Research Council, Bulletin 54 (New York, 1946), 15–52.
6. With Frederick H. Jackson,
   "A Neglected Landmark in the History of Ideas,"
   Mississippi Valley Historical Review, XXXIV (1947), 201–220.
7. "Gertrude Stein and Composition,"
   Sewanee Review, LVII (Summer, 1949), 411–424.
8. "Concept of the Artist As Exile,"
   Epoch, Vol. II, No. 4 (Winter, 1950), 277–289.
9. ": : 2 : 1, The Modern World and E. E. Cummings,"
   Sewanee Review, LXI (Spring, 1951), 206–227.
   Same, Japanese translation by Kitasono Katue in *Vou*, 36 (Tokyo, Japan, Fall, 1951), 2–7.

10. "Some Relationships between British Inductive Logic and French Impressionist Painting,"

Essays in Honor of Conyers Read, ed. Norton Downs (University of Chicago Press, 1952), 1–29, 271–273.

11. German Influence upon English Education and Science, 1800–1866,

Connecticut College Monograph #6 (New London, Conn., 1957), xii + 106.

12. "German Influence upon Scientific Instruction in England, 1867–1887,"

Victorian Studies, I (1958), 215–244.

13. "Technology and Liberal Education," 1859: Entering an Age of Crisis (Indiana University Press, Bloomington, 1959), pp. 97–112.

Appendix II

Table of Contents of
The German Influence and the
Decline of England

(The complete manuscript is on deposit in the Palmer Library, Connecticut College; a microfilm is available for inter-library loan)

Part I. The First Phase: 1815–1866
Early Intellectual Influences